A LAWYER'S GUIDE TO

Understanding Hedge Fund, Private Equity, and Venture Capital Valuation

KENNETH J. PIA, JR., SCOTT M. DEMARCO,
VLADIMIR V. KOROBOV, AND JAY E. FISHMAN

AMERICAN BAR ASSOCIATION
Family Law Section

Cover design by Mary Anne Kulchawik/ABA Design

Printed in the United States of America.

30 29 28 27 26 5 4 3 2 1

ISBN 978-1-63905-758-0

Contents

About the Authors

We thank **Kenneth J. Pia, Jr.**, **Scott DeMarco**, **Vladimir Korobov**, and **Jay E. Fishman** for serving as the principal authors of this edition. Their deep experience in business valuation—particularly in the hedge fund, private equity, and venture capital sectors—formed the foundation of this work. Each brought practical insight and technical expertise that shaped the content and structure of the book. Their contributions reflect years of leadership in the field and a shared commitment to advancing valuation understanding in legal and financial contexts.

Authors

Kenneth J. Pia, Jr., ASA, CPA/ABV, MCBA, is a lead managing director at CBIZ and leads the firm's Matrimonial Practice Group. With nearly 40 years of valuation experience, Mr. Pia has deep expertise in complex ownership interests, including those related to hedge funds, private equity, and venture capital. He is a former chair of the American Society of Appraisers (ASA) Business Valuation Committee, a member of the National Business Valuation Education Sub-Committee, and teaches nationally for the ASA accreditation program. He has testified in federal and state courts, as well as in arbitration, and serves on multiple advisory boards within the legal and valuation communities.

Mr. Pia is a charter member of the American Academy of Matrimonial Lawyers (AAML) Foundation's Forensic and Business Valuation Division where he serves as co-chair and was named to the American Academy for Certified Financial Litigators Advisory Board for New York and Connecticut. He is a frequent speaker and contributor on valuation issues involving alternative investments and closely held entities.

Scott M. DeMarco, MBA, CVA, CBA, CDFA, CPVA, is a managing director at Marshall & Stevens, where he leads the firm's Northeast Region Valuation Advisory Practice. With more than 20 years of experience, Mr. DeMarco specializes in business valuation, forensic accounting, and litigation support, including complex ownership interests in hedge funds, private equity, and closely held entities. His expertise spans matters involving matrimonial disputes, shareholder litigation, economic damages, and intellectual property valuation.

Prior to joining Marshall & Stevens, Mr. DeMarco was the managing partner of Equitable Value, LLC, which was acquired by the firm in 2024. He also brings practical experience as a technology entrepreneur, having founded and exited two software companies. Mr. DeMarco regularly speaks and writes on valuation, litigation, and the intersection of finance and technology, and has provided expert testimony in numerous state and federal court proceedings.

Vladimir V. Korobov, CPA, ABV, ASA, is a managing director at CBIZ and serves as a senior leader within the firm's National Business Valuation Group. With more than 20 years of experience, Mr. Korobov specializes in the valuation of hedge fund and private equity interests, complex partnership structures, carried interest, and intangible assets. His work supports litigation, financial reporting, estate and gift tax, and transactional engagements involving alternative investment entities.

Mr. Korobov is a frequent speaker on valuation issues related to asset management firms and has taught nationally on topics such as performance fee structures and valuation methodologies. He also serves on the Editorial Review Board of Business Valuation Review and is a charter member of the AAML Foundation's Forensic and Business Valuation Division.

Jay E. Fishman, FASA, FRICS, is managing director at Stout and has more than 40 years of experience in business valuation. Mr. Fishman has co-authored several foundational texts in the field, including *PPC's Guide to Business Valuations* and *Standards of Value*. He has provided expert testimony in courts across the United States and internationally and has taught valuation principles for organizations such as the Internal Revenue Service, the National Judicial College, and the World Bank. He is a former chairman of the ASA Business Valuation Committee and served on multiple boards of The Appraisal Foundation. Mr. Fishman sat on the Board of Trustees of the International Valuation Standards Council and received the ASA Lifetime Achievement Award in 2020 for his enduring contributions to the profession.

He is a frequent speaker at national and international conferences on valuation issues involving complex ownership structures. Mr. Fishman's work continues to shape best practices in both litigation and transactional valuation engagements.

Contributing Authors

Leo Berg, CPA, co-authored Chapter 13, "Accounting and Tax Issues Related to Hedge Funds and Private Equity Firms." He is a senior tax manager at CBIZ, where he advises asset managers on tax structuring, compliance, and financial reporting. Mr. Berg has 20 years of experience serving private equity and hedge fund clients and is a specialist in partnership taxation and fund accounting. He has held senior roles at leading accounting firms and regularly consults on complex asset management tax issues.

Lyle Kotler, CPA, co-authored Chapter 13, "Accounting and Tax Issues Related to Hedge Funds and Private Equity Firms." He is a managing director in the Alternative Investment Group of CBIZ, where he advises private equity funds, hedge funds, and investment partnerships on tax compliance and consulting matters. Mr. Kotler has more than 20 years of experience in the alternative investment industry and began his career at a Big Four firm. He is a member of the American Institute of Certified Public Accountants (AICPA) and the New York State Society of CPAs (NYSSCPA), where he serves on the Taxation of Financial Instruments and Transactions Committee.

Scott Loesch, CPA, ABV, CFE, was a contributing author to several chapters including Appendix A, "Common Terms Used in Hedge Funds and Private Equity Firms," Chapter 3, "Typical Types of Valuation Interests and Areas of Valuation," and Chapter 10, "Typical Challenges and Considerations in the Valuation of Hedge Funds and Private Equity Firms." He is a director at CBIZ specializing in business valuation, forensic accounting, and litigation support. Mr. Loesch provides valuations for privately held businesses, professional practices, and enhanced earning capacities, with a particular focus on matrimonial matters. He also conducts forensic investigations involving asset tracing and financial analysis for litigation and tax proceedings.

Adam Zoia, B.S., B.A., Hon. B.A., J.D., co-authored Chapter 11, "Reasonable Compensation for Key Managers/Principals." He is the chairman and founder of Glocap Search and chief executive officer of Glocap Tech, with more than 25 years of experience in recruiting investment professionals across private equity and hedge funds. Mr. Zoia has authored numerous articles on compensation and human capital strategy and is a frequent speaker at industry conferences.

Manuscript Editors

We extend our sincere thanks to **Jesse Keen** and **Grant Zindel** for their thoughtful editorial review and manuscript proofing. Their careful attention and professionalism were critical to the completion of this edition. We are grateful for their time, insight, and support throughout the process. Their contributions helped ensure the quality and clarity of the final work.

Foreword

Looking back at the first quarter of this 21st century, one of the fastest growing valuation niches confronting experts is the explosion in the number and size of hedge funds and private equity funds. As to hedge funds, one source indicated the number of these funds has grown from approximately 3,000 in 2000 to somewhere between 9,000 and 10,000 in 2024. A similar pattern exists for private equity funds. As a result, the demand for valuations of the entities that manage these funds (alternative asset management firms) has exploded as well. Often the purpose of these valuations intersect with the legal community.

Throughout my career in valuation, I've consistently seen attorneys encounter complex financial landscapes involving hedge funds, private equity, and venture capital. These scenarios frequently arise in litigation, transactions, tax matters, and matrimonial disputes. Yet, despite their prominence, these valuation concepts understandably remain challenging for many professionals to navigate confidently.

Recognizing this critical gap, we assembled a team of seasoned experts to produce "A Lawyer's Guide to Understanding Hedge Fund, Private Equity, and Venture Capital (HFPEVC) Valuation." Our goal was simple: to provide attorneys with clear, concise, and practical insights into the valuation processes unique to alternative asset management firms.

This handbook demystifies valuation methodologies, explains intricate fee structures and carried interest, and offers practical guidance on interpreting valuation reports effectively. It equips attorneys with essential tools for conducting comprehensive discovery, navigating complex valuation concepts specific to these entities, and developing persuasive strategies. The detailed explanations and illustrative examples are tailored specifically to enhance attorney effectiveness when dealing with complex valuation issues involving HFPEVC firms.

I am confident that our collective expertise, drawn from decades of hands-on valuation experience, will significantly enhance your practice. Consider this guide your indispensable resource whenever valuation complexities related to HFPEVC firms emerge in your legal matters.

Jay E. Fishman, FASA, FRICS
Managing Director, Stout

Introduction

The purpose of this book is to provide guidance to help understand the valuation of entities that manage hedge funds and private equity funds. Hedge funds and private equity funds are a class of pooled investments known as alternative investments.

The terms "hedge" and "private equity fund" typically elicit thoughts of complex financial algorithms, high-powered deals, and intricate ownership structures. The manager of a hedge fund or a private equity fund may have more than one type of ownership interest. Managers of more traditional investments do not typically invest alongside other investors (their customers) and receive a performance fee if the investment does well. As will be discussed in subsequent chapters of this book, it is more common, however not universal, for a manager of a hedge fund or private equity fund to invest in the fund as well as receive performance fees for their management.

Ownership interests in entities that manage hedge and private equity funds can be valued through a multi-step process:

1. Identify the components of value (e.g., ownership in the management company, performance fees, etc.).
2. Understand the entitlements of the ownership interests from a legal perspective (e.g., review the organizational chart and partnership agreements as a starting place).
3. Understand the practical aspects of how the ownership interests generate value based upon firm operations (e.g., which entity hires employees, which entity holds investments, etc.).
4. Understand the mechanics of how these entities operate.
5. Research industry and economic factors affecting ownership interests.
6. Review historical performance and assess future performance.
7. Perform the appropriate valuation methodologies for each component of value.
8. Apply discounts, where appropriate.
9. Calculate imputed taxes on the various values, when relevant.

This handbook is meant to provide a general overview regarding the valuation of economic and ownership interests in entities that manage hedge funds and private equity funds.

For the purposes of this valuation handbook, "private equity" broadly refers to pooled funds from investors that contribute capital to invest in specific situations. Often, these private equity funds are investing in private companies, but that does not exclude them from buying out public companies. Investors in private equity funds can be both retail or institutional investors and often include insurance companies, university endowments, and pension funds. Hedge funds are similar in that they also use pooled funds from investors, but they typically offer higher liquidity and use complex trading tactics as well as portfolio construction and risk management strategies to improve performance.

Private equity hedge funds and private equity funds are part of an "asset class" called alternative investments, a category that includes, among other types of investments, collateralized debt obligations (CDOs), collateralized loan obligations (CLOs), and crypto currencies.

Simplified examples will be presented herein to describe the basic valuation methodologies for entities that manage private equity and hedge funds that may be developed further and applied in real world scenarios.

Chapter 1

The History of Alternative Asset Management Firms

Introduction

The purpose of this book is to provide guidance to understanding hedge fund and private equity fund (including venture capital funds) valuation. These type of firms manage funds that are known as alternative investments.

What are alternative investments?

The question on "alternative investments" is, what are they an alternative to? We think it is best said in the CFA Institute Investment Series: Alternative Investment, which indicates the following:

> Alternative investments are a label for a disparate group of investments that are distinguished from long only,[1] publicly traded investments in stocks, bonds and cash (often referred to as traditional investments). The terms traditional and alternative should not imply that alternatives are necessarily uncommon or that they are relatively recent additions to the investment universe. Alternative investments include such assets as real estate and commodities, which arguably are two of the oldest types of investments.[2]

Entities that manage private equity and hedge funds manage what are referred to as "pooled funds." Pooled funds are funds formed from many different investors that are pooled for the purposes of investment. The most common pooled funds are traditional public stock and bond mutual funds. Examples of this are the family of funds offered by organizations like Vanguard or Fidelity. In the case of alternative investments, these pooled funds have either an investment strategy or a type of investment that makes them distinctly different from a mutual fund. Historically, the most common alternative investments are investments in what is referred to as "real assets."

1. "Long only" or "long" positions comprise investment vehicles that take long positions in securities with an aim to profit from price appreciation over time.
2. CFA Institute, *Alternative Investments* (Hoboken, NJ: John Wiley & Sons, 2021), 46.

Real assets are tangible assets: their value is based on their physical characteristics. The two most common real asset investments are real estate and commodities. Real estate has many opportunities for diversification both by type and geography. The same can be said of commodities, often classified as soft commodities like fruit, cocoa, and orange juice, and hard commodities like gold, copper, and oil.

Hedge funds and private equity funds are also classified as alternative investments. These types of funds generally do not invest in the types of tangible assets mentioned earlier but in various types of financial securities and/or financial instruments derived from them. Due to the type of investments, varying investment strategies, their private nature, and structure, they are distinctly different from traditional asset funds and funds that invest in real assets.

Hedge funds and private equity funds are not new and can trace their origins back decades. Although they may have existed in various forms before, Alfred Winslow Jones is credited with creating the first hedge fund strategy in 1949. His thesis was to buy assets that were expected to rise in the future relative to the overall performance of the market and sell short assets, or those whose price he expected to decrease. The idea was that this so-called negative correlation[3] would limit market risk and result in a portfolio of assets that were market neutral. In other words, the stocks that rose relative to the market would offset the stocks that were sold short, thereby making the risk associated with the portfolio relative to the market neutral.

Modern private equity funds have a longer history than hedge funds. The origins of private equity are often traced back to 1901, when billionaire J.P. Morgan purchased Carnegie Steel from Andrew Carnegie and Henry Phipps for a reported $480 million. Henry Phipps took the proceeds and created a private equity fund called Bessemer Trust. Though perhaps in a somewhat different form, Bessemer Trust still exists today.

Summary

This chapter introduces the concept of alternative investments and their role in the financial industry, with a focus on hedge funds and private equity funds. It begins by defining "alternative investments" as a broad category of assets and strategies distinct from traditional investments like publicly traded stocks, bonds, and cash. While alternative investments may seem

3. "Negative correlation" is when an investor buys stocks that move in the opposite direction of each other due to changes in market condition. Like the Alfred Winslow Jones funds, this strategy is used to reduce the level of risk, compared to that of the market, in their portfolios but maintain the desired return.

modern, they include some of the oldest types of assets, such as real estate and commodities, which are tangible and derive value from their physical properties. These real assets offer diversification opportunities, such as geographic or type-based variation in real estate or the classification of commodities into soft (e.g., cocoa, fruit) and hard (e.g., gold, oil) categories.

Hedge funds and private equity funds are also classified as alternative investments but differ from real assets in that they focus on financial securities and instruments rather than physical assets. These funds manage *pooled funds*, which aggregate capital from multiple investors for investment purposes. Unlike traditional mutual funds, hedge funds and private equity funds employ unique strategies, structures, and private operations that set them apart from traditional asset classes.

The chapter highlights the historical origins of hedge funds, crediting Alfred Winslow Jones with creating the first hedge fund strategy in 1949. Jones's approach involved combining long positions (buying assets expected to rise) with short positions (selling assets expected to fall), aiming to create a portfolio that was market-neutral, thereby reducing overall market risk.

In summary, the chapter provides an overview of the history and characteristics of alternative investments, emphasizing the differences between traditional and alternative asset classes. It also introduces readers to the foundational principles of hedge funds and private equity funds, setting the stage for a deeper exploration of how these firms are valued.

Chapter 2

Hedge Funds, Private Equity, and Venture Capital Funds

Hedge funds are private investment funds that manage portfolios and/or derivative positions[1] using a variety of strategies. Private equity funds are funds that invest primarily in non-traded companies, either in whole or in part. They in turn manage portfolios of these investments in a pooled fund.

Many large pension funds, endowments, family offices, sovereign wealth funds, and other investors allocate a portion of their investment capital to hedge funds and private equity funds, just as they may allocate investment capital to U.S. stock markets, emerging markets, fixed income, and so on. Despite hedge funds and private equity funds being grouped into the alternative investment asset class, the individual funds themselves may execute diverse investment strategies. For example, one hedge fund may focus on selecting undervalued U.S. publicly traded industrial companies, and another may invest in mortgage-backed securities.

One of the defining differences between hedge funds and private equity funds is that private equity funds typically invest in more illiquid investments, and hedge funds invest in securities with more liquidity. Therefore, private equity fund investments typically have a longer holding period than hedge funds. One of the impacts of this longer holding period on investors is that private equity funds generally do not allow investors to redeem their investments upon request. Hedge fund investors are typically allowed to redeem their investments in funds quarterly (due to the liquidity of the underlying fund investments), with various restrictions. For example, a provision (often referred to as a "gate provision") may restrict the timing of redemptions or halt them indefinitely at a manager's discretion, while a lock-up period denies investors access to their invested capital for a period after a new investment.[2]

---

1. Derivatives are securities whose value are derived from an underlying security, for example stock options.

2. James Chen, Gate Provision: What It Is, How It Works, Examples, reviewed by Thomas J. Catalano. *Investopedia*, https://www.investopedia.com/ (last updated Oct. 28, 2025).

Although private equity fund investors typically keep their money invested in the fund and receive their investments back when the underlying investments are exited, a growing secondary market exists in which private equity limited partnership positions can be bought or sold for liquidity and asset allocation purposes, with the buyer assuming all rights and obligations of the seller.[3] Generally, this requires the consent of the general partner (GP) of the fund. The GP may be amenable to the sale of an investor's interest for several reasons, including considering it an opportunity to develop new investor relationships and also to diversify the composition of their investors.

Hedge Funds

While there is no formal legal definition of a hedge fund, the term generally refers to an investment entity with whom investors pool their funds to be managed by an individual or a team of people based on their experience and expertise in financial investing. The fund managers derive revenue by charging fees directly to investors.

Hedge funds are diverse in their assets, investment strategies, and risk profiles. Hedge funds seek to achieve a positive return using a range of techniques such as rapid price discovery; mathematical and statistical processing; risk measurement and control techniques; and active trading in corporate equities, bonds, foreign exchange, futures, options, swaps, forwards, and other derivatives. Hedge funds and private equity funds both may use leverage (debt), which may magnify investment risk and returns. Hedge funds were initially conceived as investment vehicles that minimized the risk of declines in investment value (i.e., lower volatility); however, the term "hedge fund" can be a misnomer for many so-called funds because many hedge funds have equal or greater volatility than the overall financial markets.

Many equity (e.g., U.S. publicly traded stocks) hedge funds employ "long-only" and "long/short" investment strategies. Taking a "long" position in a company's stock means that the company's stock is purchased outright, because the investor believes that the value of the stock will appreciate and will be sold at a profit in the future. Taking a short position in a company's stock generally means that an investor borrows a company's stock and sells it at the current price, believing that the stock value will decrease. When the stock is repurchased at a lower price in the future, gains will be

3. Jochen Mende et al., "Introductory Guide to Investing in Private Equity Secondaries," *Alternative Investment Analyst Review* (Quarter 3, 2016).

realized to the extent that the sale proceeds exceed the cost to repurchase the shares (i.e., "cover" the short position).

The hedge fund management company receives a management fee typically in the range of 1% to 2% annually (paid on a quarterly basis) of assets under management (AUM). If the investment performance is positive at calendar year-end, a performance fee (also called an incentive fee) is paid from the limited partners (LPs) to the GP manager of the fund. The appreciation of each LP's investment is tracked based upon the market value of the investment as compared to the investor's high-water mark value (the highest level that a capital account or investment fund has reached). If the market value of an LP's investment is greater than the high-water mark value at year-end (or upon the LP's redemption of investment), then the performance fee percentage (typically 10% to 25%) is applied to the difference and that amount is paid to the GP. This calculation will be described in greater depth in a subsequent chapter.

Private Equity Funds

Private equity funds typically have ten-year terms (i.e., a ten-year life) with options to extend terms for additional years. In general, the goal of a private equity fund is to invest in portfolio companies during the first five years of the life of the fund, hold the investments in the fund for three to six years, and then harvest each investment hopefully at a profit during the second five years of its life. In general, private equity funds have the following stages:

- Fundraising (six months to two years)
- Investment period (five years)
- Exit period (five years)
- Final distributions/calculations and the legal end of the fund

Investors in hedge funds and private equity are LPs, though investment funds can be organized not only as limited partnerships, but also as limited liability companies, or some other legal forms of companies. In private equity funds, instead of investing all the capital upfront when the fund is set up, LPs subscribe, or commit a certain amount of capital, to the fund during the fundraising stage; the investment manager (or "management company") then sources the investments for the fund's portfolio and "calls" capital from the LPs to invest during the first five years of the fund life (i.e., the investment period). The investments are generally held for three to six years, and are then exited, hopefully at a gain. The gains from exited investments may exceed certain benchmarks. To the extent that any gains exceed these benchmarks (e.g., often an 8% preferred return to the LP), the GP of the fund may be entitled to a "carried interest" (i.e., performance fee), which is ultimately determined at the legal end of the fund's life. Carried interest will be described in greater detail in subsequent chapters.

Importantly, while carried interest may be paid as investments are exited, the ultimate amount of carried interest due to the GP is only known when the fund terminates after exiting its last investment. For example, if one investment is exited early on at a profit and carried interest is paid to the GP, but a later investment is exited at a loss, the earlier carried interest distribution may be "clawed back" from the GP and repaid to the LP. An owner in the GP entity that received the early carried interest distribution may have to literally reach into their own pocket to pay the clawback to the LP. The required amount of the clawback paid back to the LP is typically less than the original gross distribution, since the GP had to pay taxes on the original distribution.

For managing the private equity fund, the management company receives a management fee typically in the range of 1% to 2% annually of the fund's AUM. These management fees pay the operating expenses of the management company, such as investment professional salaries, office rent, insurance, and the like. Small funds may cause the management company to operate at an annual loss or breakeven with the hopes of receiving carried interest as investments are exited. Larger funds may allow the management company to generate significant profit and use those profits as the basis of the GP's investment. This is known as a fee waiver.

In most cases, the owners/organizers of private equity funds are required to invest their own funds (many times through the GP) into the funds so that they have "skin in the game." These GP investments are tracked similarly to the LP investments, with capital account statements. Capital account statements show the fair value of each investor's investment in the private equity fund under the assumption that each investment was exited at an appraised fair value (which will be defined in Chapter 4) as of a certain date, even though the LPs have no ability to monetize the underlying investments of the fund.

Venture Capital Funds

Venture capital (VC) funds are really a subset of private equity in that investments are made into a company. However, there the similarity usually ends. A useful definition of "venture capital" is as follows:

> Venture capital is the supply of equity financing to startup companies that do not have a sufficient track record to attract investment capital from

> traditional sources (e.g., the public markets or lending institutions). Startups that develop business plans require investment capital to implement those plans. However, these startup ventures often lack tangible assets that can be used as collateral for a loan. In addition, startup companies are unlikely to produce positive earnings for several years. Negative cash flows are another reason why banks and other lending institutions, as well as the public stock markets, are unwilling to provide capital to support the business plans.[4]

While the origins of VC in the United States can be traced back to as early as the whaling period, 1946 has been traditionally credited as the birth of modern VC. This is traced back to the establishment of the American Research Development Corporation (ARDC). ARDC was founded by Georges Doriot (often identified as the father of venture capitalism), Ralph Flanders (a former president of the Federal Reserve Bank of Boston), and Karl Compton (a former president of Massachusetts Institute of Technology). At the time it was a closed-end,[5] publicly traded fund located in Boston, Massachusetts. ARDC started sourcing funds from institutions like universities, insurance companies, mutual funds, and investment trusts. The firm strategically directed these investments into private companies harnessing technologies developed during World War II. From 1946 through approximately 1957, there were only four pioneering firms, joined intermittently by other investors, that practiced VC investing with some success, but no other entrants were attracted to the market.[6]

Subsequently, three watershed developments led to the popularity, management, and structure of VC funds as they exist today.

In 1958, Congress created small business investment companies (SBICs). These were created with a federal loan guarantee to private investors to provide both management assistance and venture financing for startup companies. The program was administered and regulated by the Small Business Administration. It was also during this time that these types of investors began to be referred to as "venture capitalists."[7]

---

4. Mark J.P. Anson, *Handbook of Alternative Assets*, 2nd ed. (Hoboken, NJ: John Wiley & Sons, 2006), 380.

5. In general, a closed-end fund is a type of investment fund whose portfolio is fixed at the time of the fund's formation. In contrast, open-end funds are investment funds whose net assets change as investors contribute or redeem capital.

6. Martin Kenney, "How Venture Capital Became a Component of the US National System of Innovation," *Industrial and Corporate Change* 20, no. 6 (2011): 1689.

7. The term was attributed to Arthur Rock, an early investor in startup firms. Sharon Driscoll, "Legal Matters: Arthur Rock on the Early Venture Capital Decisions That Sparked Decades of Innovation," *Stanford Lawyer* 107 (2022). Rock is also considered the father of Silicon Valley.

The second development was the formulation of an alternative organization structure: VC limited partnerships, with the founding of Draper, Gaither, and Anderson (DGA). The limited partnership has become the standard structure for investing in VC by wealthy families and institutional investors.[8]

The third significant event was in April 1973, with the founding of the National Venture Capital Association (NVCA) and a loosening of Employee Retirement Income Security Act (ERISA) regulations later in that decade that allowed investment in professionally managed VC funds by pension funds regulated by the Department of Labor under ERISA.[9]

Since then, the VC industry has continued to evolve, benefiting from the reduction in the capital gains tax rate from 50% to 28%, surviving the technology bubble at the start of this century, and eventually maturing to what it is today.

Today, VC consists of three types of investment based on the investment stage: early-stage, expansion-stage, and late-stage, depending on the development of the investment and the round of financing.

8. Anson, *supra* note 4, at 381.
9. This was known as the "prudent person" rule.

Chapter 3

Typical Types of Valuation Interests and Areas of Valuation

When valuing entities that manage hedge funds and private equity funds (including venture capital firms), it is important to understand how the funds are structured. To help with this, during the discovery process, one can request a fund structure (organizational) chart, which illustrates the relevant entities and the relationship between the entities (i.e., the flow of management fees, performance fees, ownership, etc.). These charts essentially summarize information typically found in operating agreements, offering memoranda, and other similar fund documents. These documents should be used to verify the information presented on the fund structure chart. Additionally, one can request or search for the firm's Form ADV as well as its Firm Brochure (Part 2A of Form ADV);[1] these documents will be helpful in identifying the relevant entities, services provided, assets under management (AUM), investment strategy, applicable fees, types of clients, disciplinary information, and investment risks, among other information.[2]

Equally important to understanding the hedge fund and private equity structure is understanding the types of entities and interests that are typically encountered in matrimonial litigation. These entities include the management company, general partnership entities, and limited partner (LP) interests in the fund.

Management Company Overview

Typically, hedge funds and private equity firms have a single management company. In the event there are numerous funds, there may be more than

1. Securities and Exchange Commission (SEC) Form ADV is a mandatory filing that investment advisers submit to the SEC or state regulators to disclose key information about their business, services, fees, and conflicts of interest.

2. SEC Form ADV, officially called the Uniform Application for Investment Adviser Registration and Report by Exempt Reporting Advisers, is a registration document that investment advisers must submit to the SEC and state securities authorities. It provides essential information about the advisory firm, business practices, fees, conflicts of interest, and disciplinary history.

one management company. The management entity determines the investment strategy, selects and manages the portfolio of assets, and executes trades. Management companies also oversee risk management; market funds to potential investors and handle other investor-related tasks; manage the operations of the funds, such as accounting, service provider management, and other administrative tasks; and monitor the performance of the funds, including communicating the performance to investors, generally through quarterly investor letters. Management companies generate revenue for managing a fund's AUM or investments. For example, a hedge fund may charge a 1% to 2% management fee per annum that is paid on a quarterly basis and is based upon each LP's AUM as of a stated date. As another example, a private equity firm may charge a 1% to 2% management fee per annum that is paid on a quarterly basis and is based upon aggregate investor commitments during the investment period, and contributed capital after the investment period ends. Management fee revenue is primarily used to cover operating costs such as employee compensation, technology expenses, professional fees, occupancy, and other operating expenses.

General Partner Overview

The general partner (GP) entity has legal control over the fund and is responsible for the fund's operations, regulatory compliance, and governance. The GP entity decides the overall fund structure and bears the ultimate legal responsibility for the fund's activities. While the GP has decision-making authority in connection with the fund's investments, typically the GP delegates this authority to the management company. If a hedge fund's annual performance was positive and its LPs are above their high-water mark,[3] the GP of a hedge fund is compensated at year-end through a special performance fee that is allocated from the returns earned by the LPs. A GP of a private equity firm may be compensated if the gains from exited investments exceed certain benchmarks, usually a preferred return or hurdle rate. This additional, specially allocated income is called either carried interest, an incentive fee, or a performance fee. In certain fund structures, the management company is allocated the annual performance fee or carried interest; however, this is atypical.

3. High-water mark is the highest level of value reached by a portfolio or investment account.

GP Interest and LP Interest

A GP interest refers to the ownership and economic interest that the GP entity holds directly in the fund (i.e., the GP's direct investment in the fund), and represents a share of the fund's net assets, profits, and losses. The GP interest also functions as a mechanism to align the investment managers' interest with that of a fund's LP investors. This is often referred to as having "skin in the game."

An LP is typically a passive investor—typically a high-net-worth individual or institution—who provides the majority of the funds invested capital. An LP typically has no involvement in the fund's day-to-day management or investment decisions but rather has a direct ownership interest in the fund.

Interests Subject to Valuation

In connection with entities that manage hedge funds and private equity entities, the interests that typically come up as subjects of valuation are:

- Direct fund interests (e.g., LP investments and waived fees)
- Ownership interest in the management company
- Ownership interest in the GP (i.e., special profit allocation entities)

We will discuss these interests in more detail in the following sections.

Direct Fund Interests

Direct fund interests include GP and LP interests, as discussed earlier. As will be discussed in Chapter 7, the capital account balance is a logical starting point when valuing direct fund interests. The capital account balance is evidenced by periodic capital account statements, which usually reflect the interest holder's share of the fund's net assets. These types of statements and other fund records should be requested during the discovery process.

In addition to reviewing the capital account balance, a valuation of direct fund interest should identify the fund's portfolio investments. Portfolio investments can be identified by reviewing a fund's audited financial statements, schedule of investments, or other internal records. These documents are frequently requested during the discovery process as understanding a fund's investment portfolio is necessary when valuing the other interests discussed in this chapter.

Hedge funds typically hold investments in publicly traded securities where pricing information is more readily ascertainable and there is an active market in which the investments trade. By contrast, private equity funds, including venture capital firms, generally hold illiquid investments in portfolio companies that can be challenging to value.

Ownership Interest in the Management Company

The value of an interest in a management company is generally the present value of net management fees (i.e., gross management fees minus operating expenses). Management fee income is inclusive of the fees paid to the management company for managing the fund(s), usually a percentage of AUM (for a hedge fund) or committed/contributed capital (for a private equity fund). A management entity may have other types of revenue as well and this should be examined during the discovery process. Operating expenses of the management company include, but are not limited to, compensation and benefits, payroll tax, occupancy, technology fees, data access fees, professional fees, meals and entertainment, and travel expenses.

Ownership Interest in the GP (Special Profit Allocation Entity)

The value of an interest in a GP entity is generally the present value of net performance fees or carried interest (i.e., gross performance fees or carried interest minus related expenses such as performance-based compensation). The GP can also award what is referred to as "carry points" to certain key members of the firm, including portfolio managers, which is often done on a fund-by-fund or on a portfolio company basis.

Valuing an ownership interest in GP special profit allocation entities is discussed in further detail in Chapter 9.

Purposes of Valuation

Valuations of interests in hedge funds and private equity firms are performed for a multitude of reasons, including, but not limited to:

- Tax purposes
- Transactions
- Financial reporting
- Litigation

Valuations are often completed for the following tax purposes: (1) gifting an interest, (2) conducting estate planning, (3) tax compliance, and (4) tax domicile changes.

Transactions warrant valuations when a firm grants equity to key employees as well as when admitting new partners. Additionally, a valuation will most likely also be completed when third parties make investments in the management and GP entities.

Valuations for financial reporting involve determining the fair value of illiquid/private investments for use in preparing a fund's audited financial statements.[4]

Finally, valuations of interests in entities that manage hedge funds and private equity funds are requested for a number of reasons, including litigation, such as matrimonial (divorce) litigation and business disputes.

Conclusion

In summary, the interests that frequently come up in valuations of hedge fund and private equity fund entities are direct fund interests, interests in the management entities, and interests in GP entities. The purposes for which these interests are often valued include tax, transactions, financial reporting, and litigation (including matrimonial litigation). As will be discussed later in this guide, in the valuation of these interests, it is important to understand the subject firm's organizational structure and the interests' cash flow rights and entitlements. Requesting and reviewing the appropriate documents can significantly aid in gaining this understanding.

4. The fund-level portfolio investment valuations may be less relevant for purposes of determining the value of the aforementioned interests, unless the fund's portfolio is highly concentrated.

Chapter 4

What Is "Value" in the Context of a Hedge Fund or Private Equity Firm?

The word "value" can have a host of meanings. In the context of valuing entities that manage hedge funds and private equity funds, value needs to be defined. In business valuation, defining value begins with identifying what is known as the standard of value, which is the type of value being sought. Each standard of value contains numerous assumptions that represent the type of value being utilized in a specific engagement.[1]

The standard of value is a function of the intended use or purpose of the appraisal. The appropriate standard of value is provided by the client in consultation with the appraiser. The standard of value is typically a function of law, regulation, and intended use.

In this chapter we will discuss the standard of value at two levels: (1) the type of value used by management in valuing the assets of the fund; and (2) the standard of value applicable to an interest in the management company and general partnership.

Standards of Value Used in Valuing the Assets of a Fund

As discussed earlier, hedge funds and private equity funds are a category of alternative investments. They are pooled funds in which limited partnership interests are purchased and used by the funds to make investments. To keep investors fully informed, most management companies publish quarterly and annual reports outlining the status of the funds and their investments. Depending on the vintage of the investment, the management company may, either internally or with the help of third-party valuation specialists, value the investments so the investors have some benchmark as

1. Jay E. Fishman et al., *Standards of Value: Theory and Applications*, 2nd ed. (Hoboken, NJ: John Wiley & Sons, 2013), 1.

to the rate of return on their investment. "Value" needs to be defined in this context.

There are a number of terms that define value in looking at a hedge fund or private equity fund. Internally, the management company can use the following:

Net Asset Value

Net asset value (NAV) represents the total value of the fund's assets minus its liabilities. It is commonly used for investor redemption and subscriptions, and it can be adjusted by the management company.

Fair Value (Mark-to-Market Valuation)

Fair value refers to the price that an asset would command in the marketplace, or the amount paid to transfer a liability in an orderly transaction between market participants. Hedge funds must follow Accounting Standards Codification (ASC) 820 (Financial Accounting Standards Board's (FASB's) Fair Value Measurement)[2] valuation methodologies. Assets are characterized into:

Level 1: Market prices when public market prices are available
Level 2: Models using observable inputs
Level 3: Models using unobservable inputs like information gleaned from private companies and distressed assets

Intrinsic value (fundamental value) attempts to determine the estimated inherent worth of an investment based on fundamental metrics rather than market price. This happens when it is believed that a stock is priced above or below its true value based on an analysis of its fundamental metrics.

Often, entities that manage hedge funds and private equity funds may have internally developed policies as to how the assets of the fund are valued. For example, management may decide to value any assets that have been held for less than one year at cost. It is up to the valuation specialist to understand the valuation criteria used by the management company to value the assets of the fund.

2. ASC 820 defines how fair value should be determined for financial reporting purposes.

Standards of Value Used in Valuing an Interest in Entities That Manage Hedge Funds and Private Equity Funds[3]

In many situations, the choice of the appropriate standard of value is often dictated by circumstance, objective, contract, operation of law, or other factors. For instance, what is being valued? Does the property change hands? Who are the buyer and seller?

In many instances, the choice of the standard of value may be clear, but the meaning of that standard of value is less clear. To the valuation professional, the application of a specific standard of value has significant implications regarding the assumptions, methodologies, and techniques that should be used in a valuation.

In a judicial context, the standard of value is generally set by regulations (as in estate or gift tax), by statute (as in dissent and oppression cases), by case law (as either stated or implied by divorce cases in most states), or by some combination of the above. In financial reporting, the standard is set by the Statements of Financial Accounting Standards. Next, we introduce some common standards of value.

Fair Market Value

Fair market value is perhaps the most well-known standard of value and is commonly applied in judicial and regulatory matters. Fair market value applies to virtually all federal and state tax matters, including estate, gift, inheritance, income, and ad valorem taxes, as well as many other valuation situations.[4]

Treasury regulations give the most common valuation definition of "fair market value":

> The fair market value is the price at which the property would change hands between a willing buyer and a willing seller, neither being under any compulsion to buy or to sell and both having reasonable knowledge of relevant facts.[5]

Black's Law Dictionary defines "fair market value" as "the price that a seller is willing to accept, and a buyer is willing to pay on the open market

3. Fishman et al., *supra* note 1, chap. 1, at 5–11.

4. Shannon P. Pratt and ASA Educational Foundation, *Valuing a Business: The Analysis of Closely Held Companies*, 6th ed. (New York, NY: McGraw-Hill, 2022), 28.

5. U.S. Treasury Regulation § 20.2031-1.

and in an arm's length transaction; the point at which supply and demand intersect."[6]

The willing buyer and willing seller are presumed to deal at arm's length; they are independent third parties, not specific individuals, and therefore the price arrived at will not be influenced by any special motivations or synergies of a specific buyer. Fair market value implies a market in which the buyer and seller transact and assumes current economic conditions as of the effective date of the valuation.[7]

Under fair market value, discounts may be applied to shares of a closely held company if they lack control over the corporation or lack marketability. Additionally, the property is being valued assuming a sale, regardless of whether the property actually will be sold.

Estate and gift tax cases applying fair market value provide the most frequent interpretation of the definition and application of its principles. Using these principles, fair market value has been applied in other areas. In this chapter, when used in other contexts, the terms of fair market value are discussed only when they depart from the interpretation in estate and gift tax matters.

Fair market value is the espoused standard of value used in a number of states for valuations in connection with divorce. Generally, only assets of the management company and general partnership that can be sold are considered under a fair market value standard. In addition, discounts for lack of control or lack of marketability are usually considered.

Fair Value

Fair value may be the applicable standard of value in a number of different situations, including financial reporting, appraisals for dissenting shareholders, buyouts of oppressed shareholders, fairness opinions, and divorce.

The definition of "fair value" depends on its context. For financial reporting, "fair value" is defined in relevant accounting literature and is closely akin to, but not the same as, fair market value. The definition of fair value from the FASB for financial reporting purposes is: "The price that would be received to sell an asset or paid to transfer a liability in an orderly transaction between market participants at the measurement date."[8]

This definition is similar to the one used in estate and gift tax regulations, but it does not require that buyers and sellers be as well informed as

6. Bryan A. Garner, ed., *Black's Law Dictionary*, 11th ed. (St. Paul, MN: Thomson Reuters, 2019), 1587.

7. Pratt and ASA Educational Foundation, *supra* note 4, at 29.

8. FASB, ASC Topic 820, "Fair Value Measurement."

in fair market value for estate and gift tax. While the parties are required to be uncompelled under the Treasury regulations, fair value for financial reporting purposes prohibits only a forced or liquidation sale.[9] Commentators have been clear that fair value for financial reporting purposes is not identical to fair market value as used for estate and gift tax purposes.

In judicial appraisals, fair value is a legally mandated standard that applies to specific transactions and is commonly used in matters involving dissenters, shareholder oppression, and litigation challenging the fairness of transactions. Until recently, there was no clear consensus on the definition of fair value in judicial valuations, but prevailing precedents have suggested that use of the term "fair value" distinguishes it from fair market value and the assumptions that underlie its application. While not clearly defined until the past 20 years or so, the most recent applications have established that the fair value of shares, absent special circumstances, is their pro rata portion of enterprise value. Two prominent commentators on Delaware law define fair value as the pro rata share of "the present value of the corporation's existing assets [plus] the present value of the reinvestment opportunities available to and anticipated by the firm."[10]

Investment Value

Investment value, in the nomenclature of business valuation, means the value of an asset, business, or business interest to a specific or prospective owner. Accordingly, this type of value considers the owner's (or prospective owner's) knowledge, abilities, expectation of risks and earning potential, and other factors.[11] Investment value often considers synergies available to a specific purchaser.

For example, for some companies, investment value may reflect the added value to that company related to vertical or horizontal integration. For a manufacturer, it may reflect the added value of a distributor in order to control the distribution channel of the manufacturer's particular products. For other companies, it may reflect the added value of acquiring a competitor in order to achieve the cost savings of combined operations and possibly eliminate some price competition.

For an individual, investment value considers value to the owner and typically includes a person's reputation, unique skills, and other attributes.

---

9. David Laro and Shannon P. Pratt, *Business Valuation and Federal Taxes: Procedure, Law, and Perspective* (Hoboken, NJ: John Wiley & Sons, 2011), 14.

10. Lawrence A. Hamermesh and Michael L. Wachter, "Rationalizing Appraisal Standards in Compulsory Buyouts," *Boston College Law Review* 50 (2009): 1021.

11. *Laro*, *supra* note 9, at 16–17.

For these reasons, reflecting the added value of the combination of the company's or individual's unique attributes with the subject property, investment value may result in a higher value than fair market value, which reflects the value to a hypothetical investor and may not reflect the added value to an owner or unique purchaser.

Investment value crops up primarily in the context of marital dissolutions, whether the court calls it by that name or not. It is not uncommon to have a family law court's opinion refer to a standard of value by name, but upon reading the text of the opinion, one may find that the court considered some aspects of what the business appraisal community would view as a different standard of value, often investment value. In this context, investment value usually considers the value of property not to a hypothetical buyer or seller, but to its current owner. From a business valuation perspective, when a divorce court uses investment value in this manner, the particular buyer is the current owner, and the application of value to that particular buyer translates to an investment value. Hence, investment value is often used synonymously with value to the holder.

Fair market value is impersonal, but investment value reflects the unique situation of a particular person or company. For example, while Revenue Ruling 93-12 did away with family attribution in fair market value, a minority holder who is part of a family control group may not be accorded a minority discount under the standard of investment value.

Investment value can be measured, for example, as the discounted net cash flow that a particular investor would expect a company to earn, in the way that particular investor would operate it. For a potential corporate acquirer, for example, investment value could be measured as the stand-alone value of the subject company plus any revenue increases or cost savings that the buyer would expect to achieve as a result of the synergies between the companies.

Investment value considers value from these perspectives of the potential sellers and buyers:

- The economic needs and abilities of the parties to the transaction
- The parties' risk aversion or tolerance
- Motivation of the parties
- Business strategies and business plans
- Synergies and relationships
- Strengths and weaknesses of the target business
- Form of organization of target business[12]

12. *Laro*, *supra* note 9, at 16.

Intrinsic Value

Intrinsic value is the value considered to be inherent in the property itself. "Intrinsic value" is defined by Webster's Dictionary as "being desirable or desired for its own sake without regard to anything else"[13] and by Black's Law Dictionary as "the inherent value of a thing, without any special features that might alter its market value. The intrinsic value of a silver coin, for instance, is the value of the silver within it."[14]

Intrinsic value is not the legal standard of value in any federal or state statute. Nevertheless, the phrase "intrinsic value" is found in many judicial opinions regarding business valuation, particularly in family law cases and dissenting stockholder or oppressed stockholder cases. Because it connotes the inherent value of a thing, the term "intrinsic value" has often been used synonymously with the term "investment value."

The concept of intrinsic value arises out of the literature and practice of security analysis. In fact, the most widely sold book on security analysis, Graham and Dodd's *Security Analysis*, has an entire chapter on intrinsic value.[15] Graham and Dodd define intrinsic value as "the value which is justified by assets, earnings, dividends, definite prospects, and the factor of management."[16]

According to Graham and Dodd, these four factors are the major components of intrinsic value of a going concern:

1. Level of normal earning power and profitability in the employment of assets as distinguished from the reported earnings, which may be, and frequently are, distorted by transient influences
2. Dividends actually paid or the capacity to pay such dividends currently and in the future
3. A realistic expectation about the trend line growth of earning power
4. Stability and predictability of these quantitative and qualitative projections of the future economic value of the enterprise

In general, investment practitioners now concede the existence of an intrinsic value that differs from price. Otherwise, the merit of substantial expenditures by both Wall Street and investment management organizations

13. *Webster's Third New International Dictionary of the English Language, Unabridged* (Springfield, MA: G. & C. Merriam, 1966).

14. Garner, *supra* note 6, at 1587.

15. Sidney Cottle et al., *Graham and Dodd's Security Analysis*, 5th ed. (New York, NY: McGraw-Hill, 1988).

16. *Ibid.*, 41.

for the development of value estimates on broad lists of common stocks would be highly questionable.[17]

In other words, when a security analyst says something like "XYZ stock is selling at $30 per share, but on the basis of its fundamentals, it is worth $40 per share," the $40 value is that analyst's estimate of the stock's intrinsic value, but the trading price on that date is $30 per share. If the analyst is right, the stock price may make it to $40 per share, in which case the intrinsic value would equal the fair market value.

Graham and Dodd say that "perhaps a more descriptive title for this estimated value is central value. . . . [I]ntrinsic value is in essence the central tendency in price."[18]

However, as mentioned, the term "intrinsic value" has not been restricted to securities analysis. It has been used in connection with valuations for other purposes. Here is a representative example definition from a divorce case: "The value of an item of marital property is its intrinsic worth to the parties: the worth to the husband and wife, . . . the value to the marital partnership that the court is dissolving."[19]

Intrinsic value and investment value may seem like similar concepts, but they differ in that intrinsic value represents a judgment of value based on the perceived characteristics adhering to an investment itself, while investment value is more reliant on characteristics adhering to a particular purchaser or owner.[20]

Summary

The meaning of "value" in a hedge fund or private equity fund context depends entirely on the standard chosen for the appraisal. At the fund level, managers usually report NAV, supplemented with fair value determinations under ASC 820 (Levels 1–3 inputs) or, where market signals are thin, intrinsic or fundamental value estimates derived from the investment's underlying metrics. When the appraisal shifts to the management company or general partner, the analyst must typically decide among fair market value, fair value, and investment or intrinsic value. Because each standard carries its own assumptions, legal pedigree, and methodological implications, selecting the proper yardstick is the indispensable first step in any valuation engagement.

---

17. *Ibid.*, 43.

18. *Ibid.*

19. *Howell v. Howell*, 31 Va. App. 332, 338–39, 523 S.E.2d 514 (Va. Ct. App. 2000).

20. *Woodward v. Quigley*, 133 N.W.2d 38 (Iowa 1965); Jay E. Fishman et al., *PPC's Guide to Business Valuation* (Fort Worth, TX: Thomson PPC, 2022), § 201.17.

Chapter 5

Overview of Typical Fund Management Structures and Deal Terms

Hedge funds and private equity funds generally have similar fund structures, each with nuances in legal structure and practical implementation. In their most basic sense, private equity and hedge funds both collect money from investors and then use that investor money to make investments and pay fund expenses. For our purposes, hedge funds and private equity funds may be referred to as "investment funds" for simplicity. Investor money in hedge funds and private equity funds is typically referred to as "pooled asset funds" because the investor money resides in an investment fund and each investor has a share of total capital. Investors who do not put their money into a pooled asset fund have their investments in separately managed accounts. It is more common to see traditional asset managers typically oversee separately managed investor accounts; however, hedge funds and some private equity firms may also have some separately managed accounts for large investors. In addition, special purpose entities (SPEs) or special purpose vehicles (SPVs) may be created for a select group of investors in particular investments. This will be described in greater detail later in the chapter.

Traditional investment funds most often do not restrict themselves to sophisticated investors like those who manage endowments, family offices, and sovereign wealth funds, offering to less sophisticated investors who do not meet the minimum requirements of capital, among other things, that hedge funds and private equity funds require. Traditional asset managers may be sole proprietors, offices with backroom staff and analysts, or associated with large money managers such as Merrill Lynch, Morgan Stanley, and the like. These traditional investment managers may have a separate management company that receives management and transaction fees from clients (from separately managed accounts). The actual investor money and investments generally will be held in a brokerage account at an institution instead of being pooled in a partnership (such as in hedge funds or private equity funds).

Ownership and Operational Structure

Hedge funds and private equity funds can have many different ownership structures. However, a typical ownership structure is illustrated in Figure 5.1.

Figure 5.1
Typical Private Equity and Hedge Fund Ownership Structure

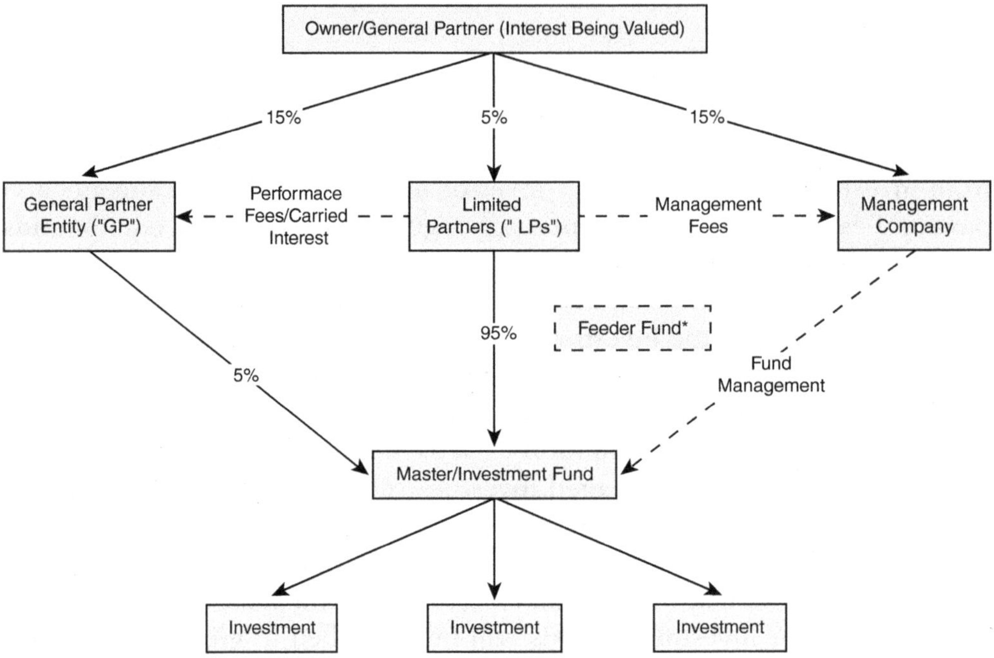

Note: In many private equity and hedge funds, limited partners may invest in feeder funds that invest the capital in a master fund, which in turn invests the pooled funds. This is referred to as a master-feeder fund structure. The ownership percentages shown in the chart are an example only.

As shown in the previous chart, an owner will typically have interests in the general partner (GP) entity (where performance fees/carried interests accrue), the management company, and direct investments in the fund(s) as a limited partner (LP). In the figure, the interest subject to valuation includes 15% interests in both the GP entity and the management company, as well as a direct LP interest in the fund. The GP has effectively contributed 5% of the total capital in the investment fund, and the LPs contributed 95% of the capital. The contributed funds are then invested at the direction of the management company.

The LPs contribute their capital directly to the investment fund through feeder funds, or other SPEs. In some cases, rather than having onshore and offshore feeder funds that feed a master fund, the onshore fund will make direct investments pari passu (i.e., in the same manner and form) with the offshore fund (rather than investing through one master fund). The contributed funds are then used to make investments in the stocks of publicly traded or privately held companies, debt, alternative assets, or other securities.

Figure 5.1 shows arrows with dashed lines (instead of solid lines) from the LPs going to the GP and management company to denote the payment or allocation of performance fees/carried interest and management fees because these fees are allocated at the fund level (either master or feeder fund level). For example, in private equity funds, carried interest is first calculated for various classes of LPs, then allocation of the carried interest is done on an LP-by-LP basis to the GP. As most investment funds are organized legally as partnerships, limited liability companies (LLCs), or another form of partnership, it is important to have a grasp of partnership accounting in valuing interests in these partnerships. While one set of financial statements is prepared for the partnership, functionally all fund income, expenses, and capital movements are tracked individually by partners for each accounting period. This becomes important when there are different classes of partners with different fund economics. For example, an investor with a relatively small investment in the fund may pay a 2% management fee and receive 20% carried interest, while a large institutional investor may pay a 1.5% management fee and receive 15% carried interest.

There are many different nuanced ownership structures that these investment funds may take, but they will have common characteristics with the chart shown in Figure 5.1. Many of these funds maintain ownership charts so that both managers and investors can see the flow of funds. At the outset of an appraisal assignment, it may be a good idea to request these charts so as to better understand the flow of funds and the documents necessary for a valuation.

General Partnership Entities

The GP entities are the controlling partners in investment funds, and in many cases receive incentive fees from the LPs. The partners in the GP entities are typically the investment managers who also have ownership interests in the management companies. Typically, the general partnership is a managing entity with the legal power to act on behalf of the fund whereas the management company is an operating entity that provides investment advice to the fund, employs investment professionals, and manages and administers the fund.[1] It is the GP that selects the management company, which works at the GP's direction. Often, they are the same individuals.

In private equity funds, GPs are typically required to contribute a certain amount of capital to the investment funds (the previously referenced "skin in the game"), either as a percentage of total capital (e.g., 1%), or as an aggregate dollar amount. Hedge fund investment managers will typically also keep a certain amount of capital in the fund for the same reason. There are no clear guidelines as to an appropriate level of skin in the game, but LPs generally prefer the investment managers to have their own money invested in the funds so that investors' and investment managers' interests are more closely aligned. For their skin-in-the-game capital investment in the funds, GP members typically are not charged for management fees or carried interests (which otherwise would be seen as paying fees to themselves since they are owners of the GP entities and the management companies).

Management Company

Hedge fund and private equity fund managers typically have one management company that directs the investments of one or multiple funds. Management companies are generally established for the sole purpose of managing a particular investment fund, family of funds, and/or separately managed accounts. They generate revenue through management agreements with investment funds that specifically state the way fees will be charged. For example, a hedge fund may charge an annualized 1.5% management fee on a quarterly basis based upon each LP's assets under management (AUM). The management company uses these management fees to pay employee compensation, rent, and various other operating expenses.

Some management companies may produce significant profits, and others may operate at losses, with much of the potential economic gain accruing to the managers through incentive fees and carried interests. LPs typically want to ensure that their interests are aligned with the economic incentives of the managers of the fund. If management fees are based upon a percentage of AUM, the management company would make more money by having more AUM, which does not necessarily occur through greater performance. For example, a hedge fund may have billions in net subscriptions from LPs in a particular year and have a negative investment return

1. Scott W. Naidech, "Private Equity Fund Formation," *Practical Law Company* (November 2011), 2, https://content.next.westlaw.com/practicallaw/document/Ibb0a1406ef0511e28578f7ccc38dcbee/Private-Equity-Fund-Formation, accessed May 1, 2020.

during the same period.[2] Management fees will have increased in that year due to the net subscriptions; however, little in incentive fees may have been paid. Over the long run there should be a positive correlation (not necessarily in the same time periods) between net subscriptions and investment rates of return. In other words, numerous years of poor returns can result in investor redemptions lowering AUM. Despite this positive correlation, LPs are typically more satisfied paying incentive fees and carried interest due to positive investment returns rather than management fees, which are not tied 100% to performance. In addition, LPs may take comfort in knowing that carried interest is only paid after all investment and management expenses have been paid, invested capital has been returned to investors, and preferred returns have been paid to the LPs. Many management companies typically generate sufficient management fees to pay employee salaries, rent, and other management company expenses, and to earn a profit on incentive fees and carried interest when investment returns are positive.

A management company's profitability over a fund's life depends on the amount of AUM that it manages, the amount of deferred or waived fees (which reduce current revenue for the management company), the life cycle stage of the fund that it manages, and other factors. Since management fees are generally based upon a percentage of AUM, and each marginal dollar in AUM does not necessarily require a linear increase in operating expenses, economies of scale may be realized by a management company. Certain investment management strategies are more labor intensive than others, but a management company with $2 billion in AUM will generally have a greater profit percentage, before owner compensation, than a fund with $50 million in AUM. However, a management company with $2 billion in AUM may not generate any current profit if the management company defers or waives a significant amount of fees as part of its capital contribution. Some management companies may operate with net losses because the investment managers hope to generate income through carried interest, which will be discussed in greater detail later in this chapter.

Co-Investments, SPEs, Side Pocket Investments, and Non-Fee-Paying Investors

In addition to GPs and LPs in an investment fund, other entities also exist, such as co-investment vehicles, SPEs, side pocket investments, and

2. LPs legally subscribe to the fund through subscription documents and then contribute their money. A redemption by an LP means that he or she withdrew his or her money from the fund, in part or whole.

non-fee-paying investors. Many times, co-investment vehicles are created in which the investment managers and others invest alongside an investment fund rather than directly in the investment fund. This may occur because the investment manager or an institutional investor wants to contribute more to a pool of investments than they otherwise would have been permitted to through the investment fund. SPEs can also be formed for reasons similar to a co-investment vehicle, but they are typically created for a single purpose (e.g., for greater investment in one particular investment).

Side pocket investments are sometimes made by hedge funds to separate illiquid assets from more liquid investments. Once an investment is put in a side pocket entity, only the investors at that time will be entitled to a share of the proceeds. By sectioning off illiquid investments into a side pocket, new LPs may be enticed to invest in the liquid investments (rather than buy into a fund with significant illiquid investments).

Provisions of Agreements and Effect on Value

The important legal documents to gather when valuing interests in entities that manage private equity and hedge funds include the partnership, LLC, and shareholder agreements (for corporations) for the management company and each fund, including the GP entities. The funds themselves will typically be formed as limited partnerships. The GP entities are generally either limited partnerships or LLCs. The management company may be an LLC, limited partnership, or corporation.

Some of the key components of a limited partnership agreement are:

- Term of the partnership (i.e., when will the partnership be dissolved, if at all)
- Allocation of net profit and loss
- Priorities for distributions of income, capital, etc.
- Management fees charged to LPs and related waivers or offsets
- Rights of partners in capital
- High-water mark provisions/loss carryforward accounts (hedge funds) and preferred rates of returns (private equity funds)
- Rights/management responsibilities of the GP
- Key person provisions (i.e., if a key person dies, becomes disabled, etc.)
- Transfers of interests
- Restrictions on withdrawal of capital

Some of the key components of a management company's or GP's ownership agreement are:

- Allocation of net profit and loss
- Distributions of income, capital, etc.
- Allocations of carried interests/incentive fees to partners (i.e., vesting terms, who determines the allocations, etc.)
- Transfers of interests
- Withdrawal rights
- Management and control

The private placement memorandum (PPM) for each fund will also provide summaries of the key provisions of the investment funds. PPMs are provided to prospective investors and include investment management biographies, investment strategies expected to be employed, historical investment returns, investment risks, and management fees, as well as various other items. PPMs help to protect the GPs from liability and inform the LPs of the risks of the investment.

Investment Fund Tax Returns

Private equity and hedge funds that are domiciled offshore, such as in the Cayman Islands, are not required to file U.S. federal tax returns. Onshore funds, United States-based management companies, and GP entities are required to file U.S. federal tax returns. However, the onshore investment funds' tax returns will likely not be as critical as each fund's financial statements. The tax returns for the investment funds will show taxable income and gains/losses but will not show economic income and gains/losses. For example, if an investment fund has two investments that have appreciated in value and one is sold in a particular year, the realized capital gain will be reported on the fund's tax return, but the unrealized gain on the second investment will not be reported on the tax return. The financial statements will likely show the gains for both investments, which is a truer picture of the economic performance of the fund.

Management Company Tax Returns

Conversely, a management company's tax return will likely be critical to the valuation of a management company since audited financial statements are typically not prepared for these types of entities. The owners in a management company are usually insiders who have insight into the inner workings of the finances of the company and investment funds, so they do not usually require audited financial statements. The tax returns may be prepared on an accrual or cash basis of accounting. The accrual basis of accounting means that revenues are recorded when services are rendered, and expenses are recorded when incurred. The cash basis of accounting means that revenue and expenses are recorded when cash is exchanged, regardless of when earned or incurred. The tax return will specify which accounting method was utilized. It is typically preferred that accrual basis income statements and balance sheets are utilized in a valuation, which means that the valuator may need to request internally prepared financial statements on an accrual basis.

For valuation purposes, historical expenses will also need to be analyzed to forecast future expenses. Certain expenses will be more fixed in nature (e.g., accounting fees), and other expenses will vary more with the size of the company (e.g., compensation). A breakdown of compensation into base and bonus compensation is important for forecasting future non-owner employee compensation.

Financial Statements

The private equity and hedge fund financial statements are important to the valuation of the various ownership interests in the funds and management company. Audited financial statements are typically prepared for most investment funds, but investors in small funds may not require them. The balance sheet will be the first financial schedule in the financial statements. In most cases, the investments held by the fund will be stated at fair value.

The Financial Accounting Standards Board (FASB) has adopted the "fair value" standard in determining the value of private equity and hedge fund investments for financial reporting purposes. FASB Accounting Standards Update (ASU) Topic 820, Fair Value Measurement, defines "fair value" as the amount that would be received to sell an asset or paid to transfer a liability in an orderly transaction between market participants at the measurement date. Fair value is similar to fair market value, but differences may exist, as discussed in Chapter 4: fair market value focuses on hypothetical buyers and sellers, whereas fair value focuses on the price that would be received by the holder of the investment.

The audited financial statements of private equity and hedge funds use the fair value standard in determining the value of each investment. If investments are not publicly traded securities, the private equity fund will have valuations performed on its investments following guidelines issued by FASB. The fund's balance sheet shows the aggregate fair values of the investments (disclosing the cost of the investments also), and the statement of investment (SOI) details the cost and fair value of each portfolio investment.

Since investment funds carry their investments at fair value, the GP and LPs' (as a class) capital account balances are also stated at fair value. The statement of changes in partners' capital shows the movements in GP and LPs' capital for the reporting period. Any accrued or reversal of accrued carried interest will be disclosed in this statement.

The notes to the financial statements provide especially useful information for valuation purposes. The first note in a financial statement describes how the investment fund is organized, stating the names of the various entities associated with the fund such as the GP and management company, the term of the partnership (i.e., fund life), and the purpose of the fund. Some funds disclose the total commitment and the GP's commitment in this note as well. Additional key notes to the financial statements are the allocations of profits and losses (i.e., determination of carried interests, performance fees, etc.), related party transactions (e.g., management fees), and the investment rate of return for the periods under review.

Capital Account Statements

Private equity and hedge funds provide capital account statements to investors on a regular basis (e.g., monthly, quarterly, etc.). In most cases, the capital account statements will be prepared on a Generally Accepted Accounting Principles (GAAP) basis that utilizes the "fair values" of the underlying investments. Therefore, the investors' capital account statement values should conform to the audited fund financial statements.

Private equity fund capital account statements can take various forms, but they are generally attempting to communicate the investor's (1) amount of committed capital, (2) unfunded capital commitment, (3) appreciation/depreciation/investment return, and (4) capital account value. Figure 5.2 is an example of an LP's capital account statement in a private equity fund. Section #1 shows that the investor committed $1 million to the fund, contributed $950,000, and had an unfunded capital commitment of $50,000. With 95% ($950,000 of $1,000,000) of the capital "called" and invested, the remaining $50,000 (5%) may not be called since most private equity funds leave some amount of capital uncalled.

Figure 5.2

Example of an LP's Capital Account Statement

Section #1	
Committed capital	$ 1,000,000
Capital contributions	(950,000)
Unfunded capital commitment	$ 50,000
Section #2	
Invested capital of current investments	$ 750,000
Disposition of capital from realized investments	200,000
Realized gain from investments	100,000
Unrealized appreciation from investments	150,000
Distributions	(300,000)
Fair value capital accounts as of June 30, 2019	$ 900,000

Section #2 of the capital account statement shows a historical perspective of the LP's investment in the private equity fund from inception to June 30, 2019. The statement delineates realized capital gains from unrealized capital gains. A realized capital gain (or loss) means that the investment was sold and generated a gain or loss. An unrealized capital gain (or loss) means that the private equity fund still holds the investment, and the investment value will continue to fluctuate until it is sold. This simplified example excludes other items possibly present on a capital account statement, such as income (dividends), expenses, and so on.

In Section #2, $750,000 of capital was invested in investments as of June 30, 2019, and $200,000 of capital had been realized (sold). The $200,000 of realized capital generated $100,000 in realized gains. The remaining $750,000 of invested capital generated $150,000 in unrealized gains as of June 30, 2019. The LP received a distribution of $300,000 (the $200,000 in realized investment capital and $100,000 in realized gains). The net effect of these figures is a $900,000 fair value capital account balance, which is composed of $750,000 of invested capital and $150,000 in unrealized gains.

The following example is similar to the prior one, but the following shows a GP's capital account statement with accrued carried interest and a clawback. The GP was allocated $4 million in realized carried interest and $100,000 in realized gains (from the $200,000 in realized capital). The $4.3 million ($4 million carried interest, $200,000 in realized capital, and $100,000 in realized gains) was distributed to the GP, but due to the performance of the remaining unrealized investments in the private equity fund, $1 million in "unrealized appreciation—carried interest" was clawed back from this GP and reallocated to the LPs. Unfortunately for this GP, the $4 million in previously realized carried interest was distributed, which means that the $1 million clawback of carried interest reduced the capital account value to *negative* $100,000. If the fund were fully liquidated as of June 30, 2019, the GP would have to reimburse the fund for $100,000 (with an adjustment for taxes previously paid by the GP).

Figure 5.3

Example of a GP's Capital Account Statement

Section #1	
Committed capital	$ 1,000,000
Capital contributions	(950,000)
Unfunded capital commitment	$ 50,000
Section #2	
Invested capital of current investments	$ 750,000
Disposition of capital from realized investments	200,000
Realized gain from investments	100,000
Unrealized appreciation from investments	150,000
Realized gains—carried interest	4,000,000
Unrealized appreciation—carried interest	(1,000,000)
Distributions	(4,300,000)
Fair value capital accounts as of June 30, 2019	$ (100,000)
	(in clawback)

Hedge fund capital account statements are typically easier to interpret than private equity capital account statements since they more closely resemble a brokerage account statement. A hedge fund capital account statement will generally show the beginning period market value (e.g., beginning of quarter), allocated income and gains (losses), and ending market value. A period investment rate of return will also typically be shown.

Fees Generated by Private Equity and Hedge Funds

In the setup of the private equity and hedge fund ownership structure, the key organizers of the funds establish the fees that are to be paid by the funds to the management company and GP entity. The management company and GP entity are typically owned predominantly by the same people.

For example, the management company may be owned by five individuals, and the GP entity, which receives carried interest and incentive fees, is typically also owned by the same five individuals. However, other employees may also own a share of the carried interest and incentive fees paid to the GP.

As stated earlier, in both private equity and hedge funds, the management company receives management fees based upon AUM. If the investment funds perform well, then performance fees (carried interests at private equity funds, and performance or incentive fees at hedge funds) are paid to the managers of the funds (in most cases). These fees are paid either to the management company directly or through an allocation to the GP. Private equity funds that invest primarily in real estate or related real estate loans may call the performance fees the "promote" rather than carried interest.

The investment funds may earn other types of fees, such as transaction fees, which will briefly be discussed herein.

Management Fees

Hedge funds and private equity funds pay management fees to a management company, typically based upon each investor's AUM as of a certain date. Management fees may be paid in advance every six months, quarterly, or monthly. Most funds pay a quarterly management fee. As stated previously, most private equity funds have two distinct periods of time: the investment period and the harvest period. During the investment period the fund managers are "calling" capital from LPs and making investments. Management fees are typically calculated as a percentage of committed capital during the investment period. After five years or so, the harvest period begins, at which time the primary focus of the private equity fund is to realize investments. During the harvest period, management fees are typically calculated as a percentage of invested capital (i.e., the cost of the remaining fund investments (usually referred to as a fee step-down)).

Hedge funds typically invest in more liquid investments, so the publicly traded prices of the underlying investments are used as the starting point for AUM. Each investor's capital account is then calculated based on the market level of AUM, and the management fee is charged to each investor as a percentage of the investor's capital account.

Transaction Fees

While a traditional investment manager may keep 100% of the transaction fees, private equity management companies typically share or offset the transaction fees with the LPs who are invested in the private equity fund being managed.

Private Equity Fund Carried Interest

Private equity firms typically call the performance fees that are allocated to GPs a "carried interest." Most private equity funds have a hurdle rate (an annual internal rate of return (IRR), also called a preferred return) that must be allocated to the LPs before carried interest is paid to the investment managers (usually as GPs) of the fund. The annual IRR has historically been more than 10% for private equity funds as a whole, but individual funds deviate from that rate.[3] In recent years, many private equity funds provide an 8% to 9% preferred return to LPs, meaning that no carried interest is allocated until the preferred return is exceeded. In addition, funds may have a catch-up provision for the GPs. LPs receive the initial distributions from the funds until they recover their contributed capital and receive the preferred return. At that point, a catch-up provision would allow the GP to receive all subsequent distributions until the cumulative profits are split according to the agreed upon LP/GP allocation (typically 80/20). Following that, profits are distributed as per the LP/GP allocation.

When an investment is exited, the sale proceeds are run through a "waterfall" as outlined in the private equity fund's ownership agreement, PPM, and financial statements. The total amount due to the LP is first determined, and then that total amount is reallocated according to the priorities of distribution (like a waterfall flows down). Figure 5.4 shows a hypothetical investment exit and reallocation of proceeds.

Figure 5.4

Hypothetical Example of a Waterfall Distribution

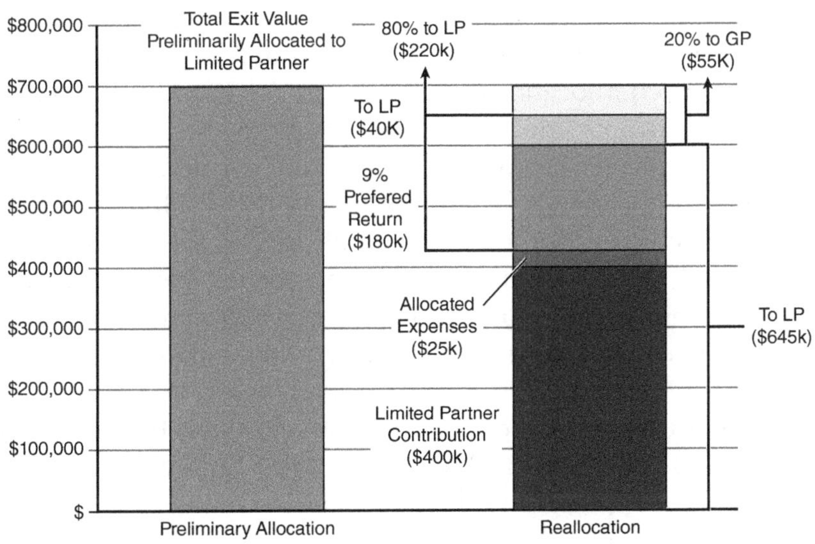

3. Cambridge Associates, "US Private Equity (Legacy Definition) Index and Selected Benchmark Statistics," September 30, 2019.

Figure 5.4 shows the preliminary allocation of $700,000 to an LP (based upon the LP's pro rata share of the fund) from an exited investment. The $700,000 is then reallocated to the LP and GP. The LP first receives an allocation equal to his or her contribution toward the investment ($400,000). Second, the LP receives a credit for the allocated share of fund expenses ($25,000). The LP then receives an allocation based upon a 9% preferred return on his or her contributions to the fund ($180,000). Lastly, the GP receives an allocation equal to 20% ($55,000) of the sum of the (1) preferred return ($180,000), (2) allocation of profit to the LP ($40,000), and (3) allocation of the 20% to the GP ($55,000); 20% of $275,000 ($180,000 + $40,000 + $55,000) equals $55,000.

In the previous hypothetical example, if the LP does not receive an allocation equal to at least the 9% preferred return, then a potential clawback is created, and the GP loses a portion of previously allocated carried interest. The preceding example is a simplified hypothetical overview, and the actual allocations and reallocations are specifically detailed in each fund's limited partnership agreement. However, the example clearly shows that the carried interest allocated to the GP is much riskier than an LP's investment. LPs receive significant compounded preferred returns, and the GPs only receive carried interest to the extent that fund performance exceeds the preferred returns.

Hedge Fund Incentive/Performance Fees

The investment professionals at a hedge fund receive an incentive/performance fee if at the end of an annual measurement period the investments allocated to an LP have appreciated. In some cases, a hedge fund may also have a preferred return similar to a private equity fund. A capital account is kept for each LP in which allocations are made for the market values of investments, expenses, income, and so on, for specific periods of time. In a very general sense, if a partner's capital account value has appreciated at the end of the year, then a percentage of that appreciation is reallocated from the LP capital account to the GP (or a fee is paid directly to the management company). However, if an LP's capital account depreciates from the beginning of the year to the end of the year, no incentive fees are paid until the capital account appreciates above the highest prior year's balance (the high-water mark).

Figure 5.5 shows the timeline of an LP's initial $100 investment on December 31, 2016, depreciation below the $100 high-water mark in 2017 and 2018, and then appreciation to $120 as of December 31, 2019.

Figure 5.5

Hypothetical Example of a High-Water Mark

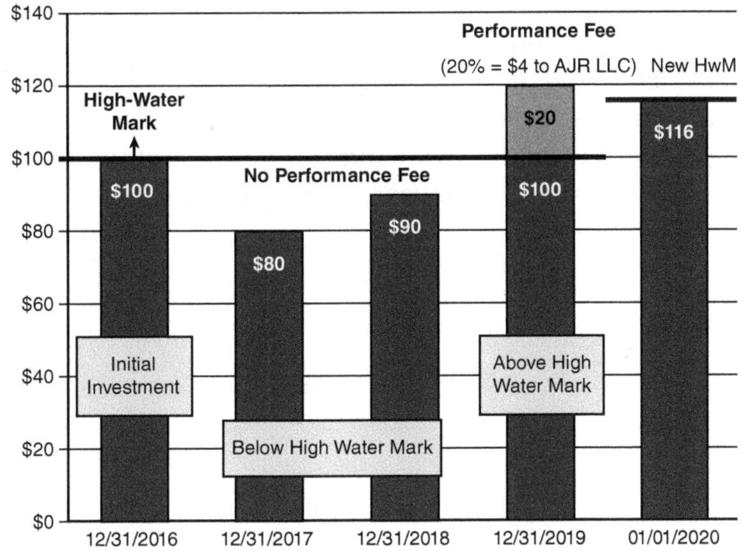

In 2017 and 2018, no performance fees were paid because the high-water mark was equal to the $100 initial investment. Once the value increased above $100, to $120, a performance fee of $4 (20% of $20) was paid to the GP. The new high-water mark after the payment of the $4 performance fee was $116 as of January 1, 2020. If the capital account value is above $116 as of December 31, 2020, then 20% of the appreciation above $116 will be paid to the GP as a performance fee.

Summary

In summary, hedge funds and private equity funds pool investors' money, typically using limited partnership or similar pass-through structures. A GP sponsors the fund, contributes a share of the fund's capital, and usually delegates the day-to-day management responsibilities to a management company. The GP is usually the entity that earns incentive fees (or carried interest) based on the investment fund's performance. Management companies earn management fees, which are usually expressed as a percentage of AUM or capital commitments. Based on their respective roles within the hedge fund or private equity fund firm's organizational structures, the GP is usually profitable when the investment fund performs well (i.e., when the

GP earns incentive fees (carried interest)), but the management company's profitability depends on the size of the fee-paying AUM. The rights and obligations of various parties within the investment firm's organizational structure are typically memorialized in the entities' governing documents that should be requested and reviewed as part of the valuation process. In addition to the entities' governing documents, counsel and experts should also consider requesting and reviewing the funds' audited financial statements, the entities' income tax returns, and capital account statements.

Chapter 6

Overview of Typical Valuation Approaches and Methodologies

While most private equity and hedge funds have similar terms in their ownership agreements and comparable operating structures, they all have some degree of variation that will affect the valuation analyst's chosen valuation method.

General partners (GPs) receive performance fees, or carried interest, from the limited partners (LPs) based on certain criteria, and potentially cash flows generated by fees received by the fund's management company. Using Figure 5.1 from Chapter 5 as an illustration, the components of value of the ownership interest can be segmented into the following:

- **Capital value**: The owner's pro rata share of market value of invested capital (as allocated to the GP entity, as well as to the owner's direct limited partnership interest, which may be through a co-investor entity)
- **Management company value**: The owner's pro rata share of the value of the management company
- **Performance fee/carried interest value**: The owner's share of the GP's carried interest or incentive fees

Allocating value to each owner can be a complex undertaking, and it is done differently in private equity than for hedge funds. For example, a typical private equity fund will have a previously described waterfall distribution that determines how an LP's total value is allocated among the GPs and LPs. The waterfall is recalculated at each reporting date, such as for quarterly reporting to investors, and each time a portfolio company is exited.

These various components of value can be appraised through use of traditional valuation approaches. For example, the discounted cash flow method can be applied under the income approach, in which forecasts are prepared or utilized from company management of capital flows and assets under management (AUM) to forecast management fees and performance fees/carried interests. These forecasted fees are then discounted to present value. Similarly, the market approach may be applied using valuation multiples derived from guideline transaction data or guideline public companies, which are then applied to the subject company. Adjustments for discounts and/or premiums may need to be applied to arrive at the value of the subject interest.

Alternatively, account statements prepared by investment funds are typically utilized as the starting point to appraise capital account values. When appropriate, adjustments would then be made, such as discounts for lack of marketability,[1] and lack of control, to arrive at the fair market value of the capital account. The details of these various valuation approaches and methodologies will be described in subsequent chapters.

1. In this guide the authors use "marketability" and "liquidity" interchangeably.

Chapter 7

Valuation of Limited Partnership Direct Fund Interests

Hedge Funds v. Private Equity Funds

When valuing investment fund interests, many appraisers often use reported "fair value" of the capital account balances as a default option (which may be subject to certain discounts). However, considerations in the valuation of direct fund interests differ materially between hedge funds and private equity funds.

Given the fact that hedge funds are typically open-ended funds, their investors have redemption rights; thus, a hedge fund investor's reported capital account balance is usually a logical and appropriate starting point in the valuation of the hedge fund interest.

Unlike hedge funds, however, private equity funds are closed-end funds, and their investors typically do not have explicit redemption/withdrawal rights. Private equity investors typically have to wait many years to realize the total value of their fund interests through distributions. Although private equity funds usually provide periodic statements to their investors showing each investor's respective share of the fund's net asset value (NAV) as of the statement's date on a fair value basis, the reported NAV reflects a hypothetical assumption that the fund's assets are sold or realized at their values as of the account statement measurement date (e.g., December 31, March 31, etc.) and the investors receive their share of the sale proceeds. However, except for very limited and specific situations,[1] this hypothetical assumption does not reflect that (1) the reported NAV may not be realized uniformly for many years, (2) over time, the value of the assets may change positively or negatively, and (3) the pattern of the fund investors' cash flow

1. For example, when an investment fund is near the end of its term, and there is a reasonable expectation that any remaining assets and liabilities of the fund will be monetized/settled at their reported values. In addition, sometimes the general partner (GP) may give the limited partner (LP) investors permission to sell their LP interests in a secondary market, as discussed later in this chapter.

may be different from the projected cash flows that the fund manager used to value portfolio investments as of the statement's date. Given these issues, a discounted cash flow method based on the fund-level cash flow[2] is the methodology most consistent with valuation theory when valuing interests in a private equity fund.

For illustration purposes, let's review an example of a private equity fund that has a general partner (GP) and one limited partner (LP). The fund's capital commitments total $1,000,000, an 80% share of which are the LP's. As of today, 70% of the commitments, or $700,000, has been called and invested in two portfolio companies, and the remaining commitments will be used to invest in one more portfolio company next year. The fund has an investment return goal of a 2.0x multiple on invested capital (MOIC).[3] The GP will receive a carried interest of 20% of the profits. Again, for illustration purposes, we assume no hurdle rate and a European waterfall[4] for allocation of portfolio distributions. The current value of the portfolio investments is $910,000, which represents an unrealized MOIC of approximately 1.3x. Each portfolio investment is expected to be held for three years before it is sold. These and other pertinent assumptions are summarized in Figure 7.1.

Figure 7.2 summarizes the fund's projected cash flow and an allocation of the projected proceeds from sales of the fund's three portfolio investments to the LP.

Figure 7.3 presents an application of the discounted cash flow method (i.e., a calculation of the present value of the LP's projected cash flow).

However, this is where economic theory and practical considerations may clash. Application of the discounted cash flow method usually requires access to certain fund-level information, like projections, and time-consuming modeling of future cash flows. Thus, while this method may be easier to apply to value interests held by investment managers of private equity firms (or in conjunction with valuing a GP interest in the fund, as is typically the case with "vertical slice" valuations performed for estate planning purposes), who have complete access to information, it is much more challenging (and often impractical) to use the discounted cash flow method to value fund interests held by a fund investor. This is because the fund's investors and the investment firm's employees/junior partners[5] do not typically have access to

2. Here, the fund-level cash flow represents the projected cash flow of a private equity fund that reflects expected capital calls for investments and fees, proceeds from disposition of portfolio investments, and allocation of the expected disposition proceeds between the fund's GP and LPs/investors.

3. 2.0x multiple means the investment will be exited at two times its cost.

4. See Appendix A for definition.

5. Here, junior partners are often senior investment or management professionals who have carried interest entitlements and share in a management entity's profits via bonuses

Figure 7.1
Illustrative Fund Commitments, Contributions, and MOIC Profile

	Committed Capital		Capital Called	Remaining Commitments
	Amount	**% of Total**	**70%**	
Limited Partner (LP)	$ 800,000	80%	$ 560,000	$ 240,000
General Partner (GP)	$ 200,000	20%	$ 140,000	$ 60,000
Total	**$ 1,000,000**		**$ 700,000**	**$ 300,000**
GP Carried Interest		20%		
LP Preferred Return		None		
Management and Other Fees		None		
Fund's Target MOIC, [a]		2.0x		
Current Date		Y+0		
Investments Made	**Investment Date**	**Invested Capital**	**Current Values**	**MOIC, [a]**
Portfolio Company 1	Y-1	$ 350,000	$ 525,000	1.5x
Portfolio Company 2	Y+0	$ 350,000	$ 385,000	1.1x
Total		$ 700,000	$ 910,000	1.3x

[a] MOIC: a multiple of invested capital (i.e., current values divided by invested capital).

information necessary for the valuation analysis. Figure 7.4 highlights some of the typical differences in information access among the four interest holder categories.[6]

In addition to the information access issues, application of the discounted cash flow method presents other practical challenges. Here are some of them:

If the valuation is being performed for purposes of a litigated matter, jurisdictional nuances should be considered by the valuation expert (i.e., the applicable standard of value, applicable valuation date, consideration of personal goodwill, application of discounts, etc.). The valuation expert should also determine whether the analysis should consider the impact of taxes in a potential sale of the interest.

---

or profits interest allocations, but who ultimately do not control any aspects of the firm's operations.

6. Figure 7.4 is based on the presentation by Kyle S. Garcia, CFA, ASA-BV/IA, CPA/ABV, and Vladimir Kolobov, CPA, ABV, ASA, at the 2024 ASA International Conference in Portland, Oregon, titled "Complex Valuation Issues in Litigation."

Figure 7.2
Fund-Level Cash Flow

	Historical		Projected, [a]				
	Y-1	Y+0	Y+1	Y+2	Y+3	Y+4	Totals
Portfolio Company 1	$ (350,000)			$ 700,000			$ 350,000
Portfolio Company 2		(350,000)			700,000		350,000
Portfolio Company 3, [b]			(300,000)			600,000	300,000
Total	**(350,000)**	**(350,000)**	**(300,000)**	**700,000**	**700,000**	**600,000**	**1,000,000**
LP's Cash Flow:							
Gross Proceeds, [c]			–	560,000	560,000	480,000	1,600,000
Less: Return of Capital			–	(560,000)	(240,000)	–	(800,000)
Profit Subject to GP Carried Interest			–	–	320,000	480,000	800,000
Less: Carried Interest, 20.0%			–	–	(64,000)	(96,000)	(160,000)
Net Profit to LP			$ -	$ -	$ 256,000	$ 384,000	$ 640,000
LP's Net Projected Pretax Cash Flow:							
Capital Contributions			(240,000)	–	–	–	(240,000)
Return of Capital			–	560,000	240,000	–	800,000
Distributions, Net of Carried Interest			–	–	256,000	384,000	640,000
Net Projected Pretax Cash Flow			**$ (240,000)**	**$ 560,000**	**$ 496,000**	**$ 384,000**	**$ 1,200,000**
LP's Invested Capital Tracker:							
Invested Capital, BoP	$ –	$ 280,000	$ 560,000	$ 800,000	$ 240,000	$ –	$ –
Contributions, [d]	280,000	280,000	240,000	–	–	–	800,000
Return of Capital	–	–	–	(560,000)	(240,000)	–	(800,000)
Invested Capital, EoP	**$ 280,000**	**$ 560,000**	**$ 800,000**	**$ 240,000**	**$ –**	**$ –**	**$ –**

[a] Each portfolio company is assumed to be held for three years and sold at the fund's target MOIC of 2.0x.

[b] Portfolio Company 3 is assumed to be acquired next year for the amount of the remaining capital commitments of $300,000.

[c] Gross proceeds are calculated as a product of the projected proceeds from a portfolio company sale and LP's share of total capital commitments. For example, for Y+2 gross proceeds to LP would be $700,000 x 80.0% = $560,000.

[d] LP's capital contributions are 80% of the fund's total investment in a portfolio company. For example, for Portfolio Company 1, the LP's capital contribution is 80% of $350,00 or $280,000.

Figure 7.3
Discounted Cash Flow Method

	Y+1	Y+2	Y+3	Y+4	Totals
Net Projected Pretax Cash Flow	$ (240,000)	$ 560,000	$ 496,000	$ 384,000	$ 1,200,000
Less Income Tax, [a]			(60,928)	(91,392)	(152,320)
After-Tax Cash Flow	**(240,000)**	**560,000**	**435,072**	**292,608**	**1,047,680**
Present Value Factor, [b]	0.8696	0.7561	0.6575	0.5718	
Present Values	**$ (208,696)**	**$ 423,440**	**$ 286,067**	**$ 167,300**	**$ 668,111**
Sum of Present Values of Cash Flow					
Tax-Effected					**$ 668,111**
Not Tax-Effected					**$ 760,426**

[a] Assumed long-term capital gains tax on net distributions in excess of return of capital at the federal long-term capital gains tax rate of 23.8% and assuming no state income tax.

[b] Assuming a discount rate of 15.0% and end-of-year discounting convention.

Figure 7.4
Access to Information for Interest's Holder

	Access to Information for Interest's Holder			
Frequently Requested Information	**Founder / Principal**	**Junior / Non-controlling Partner**	**Employee**	**3rd Party Fund Investor**
Prospectus / Offering Memorandum	Yes	Usually	Usually	Yes
Investor reports / updates / presentations	Yes	Usually	Usually	Yes
Historical fund performance	Yes	Usually	Usually (if part of offering materials)	Yes (if part of offering materials)
Portfolio company valuations	Yes	Not typically	No	No
Top employees' compensation (including carry allocations)	Yes	Not typically	No	No
Budgets / forecasts / projections	Yes	Not typically	Not typically	No
Financial statements	Yes	Usually	Not typically	No
Partnership agreements / employment and management contracts	Yes	Limited access to select documents (for example, the fund's LPA)	May have limited access to select documents	Usually has access to the fund's LPA

Given the aforementioned challenges in applying the discounted cash flow method (and often cost considerations), appraisers often default to using capital account balances when dealing with private equity fund interests.[7]

Investor's Capital Account Balance

Core issues in valuation of partnership interests in investment funds are typically (1) whether or not the reported balance of the investor's capital account on a given date is representative of the interest's fair market value, and (2) if it is not, what adjustments may be necessary to convert the reported balance into fair market value.

In the United States, domestic (i.e., onshore) investment funds are typically structured as limited partnerships. The fund's GP is tasked with maintaining a capital account for each investor that keeps track of the investor's capital contributions and distributions, and the investor's share of the fund's investment income, gains, losses, and expenses.[8] The capital account may be maintained on a tax basis, Generally Accepted Accounting Principles (GAAP) (i.e., mark-to-market) basis, or both, and the differences between the two bases of presentation can be material, as Figure 7.5 illustrates.

Figure 7.5

Comparison of Capital Account Presentations

	Tax Basis	GAAP Basis	Difference
Capital, Beginning			$ –
Contributions	$ 1,000	$ 1,000	
Current Period Realized Gains (Losses)	100	100	–
Current Period Expenses	(50)	(50)	–
Unrealized Gains (Losses)	–	200	200
Distributions	(30)	(30)	–
Current Period Expenses Non-deductible for Tax Purposes	10	–	(10)
Capital, Ending	**$ 1,030**	**$ 1,220**	**$ 190**

7. The authors' consensus is that the difficulty of performing an analysis should not be an excuse for not applying a method that is appropriate under the circumstances, but the authors acknowledge that, in practice, circumstances often arise where relying on a mark-to-market capital account balance may be an appropriate shortcut.

8. For a detailed discussion of a capital account in a partnership and related tax issues, refer to Chapter 13.

Continuing with our earlier example of the private equity fund, Figure 7.6 compares the resulting balances of the LP's capital account under various presentation bases.

Figure 7.6
Illustrative Comparison of Capital Account Values

	Tax Basis	Mark-to-Market Basis	Value, Tax-Effected	Value, Not Tax-Effected
LP's Capital Account	$ 560,000 [a]	$ 694,400 [b]	$ 668,111 [c]	$ 760,426 [d]

[a] Tax Basis is presumed to equal the LP's capital contribution to date, as shown in Figure 7.1.

[b] The mark-to-market basis represents the LP's 80.0% share of the current reported value of the fund's two portfolio investments of $910,000 shown in Figure 7.1, net of the GP's 20.0% carried interest in the appreciation.

[c] Value represents the present value of the expected remaining capital contributions and future proceeds from disposition of portfolio investments, as calculated using the discounted cash flow method and illustrated in Figure 7.3. The present value is net of tax (i.e., the capital gains tax is presumed to be paid in the year(s) when the fund disposition of portfolio investments, as calculated using the discounted cash flow method and illustrated in Figure 7.3). The present value does not consider taxes on gains from future disposition of portfolio investments.

[d] Value represents the present value of the expected remaining capital contributions and future proceeds from disposition of portfolio investments, as calculated using the discounted cash flow method and illustrated in Figure 7.3. The present value does not consider taxes on gains from future disposition of portfolio investments.

Given the potential magnitude of the presentation differences in the capital account balance, if the balance is presented on a tax basis, appraisers should attempt to obtain other relevant information (e.g., the fund's GAAP-basis audited financial statements, investor letters/reports, etc.) that could provide a reasonable basis for determining the fair market value of the capital account.

Discounts on Fund Interests

Because interests in hedge funds and private equity funds are interests in private investment partnerships, they often warrant consideration of the same or similar types of discounts that appraisers apply to determine fair market value[9] of an interest in a closely held entity, although application of the discounts to the fund interests may be more nuanced.

9. The authors recognize that some jurisdictions use fair value as the standard of value or specifically exclude minority and/or marketability discounts even when applying the fair market value standard. However, the exclusion of the discounts may be nuanced (i.e., although typical minority and marketability discounts are not allowed, other discounts that are related to the specific attributes of an asset may still be applied).

A Discount for Lack of Control

Application of the discount for lack of control to the direct fund interests is a somewhat controversial issue. Appraisers who apply this discount believe that because an LP of the fund does not have management powers and control over the fund, including the composition of the investment portfolio, the LP's interest is akin to an LP interest in a family limited partnership (FLP). Fair market values of LP interests in FLPs are routinely reduced by a discount for lack of control; thus, the same logic and approach should be applied to the fund interests. These appraisers often point to (1) price-to-NAV discounts for closed-end funds and (2) research that suggests that conglomerates tend to trade at a discount to the sum-of-the-parts values of their component businesses as market evidence that portfolios of securities tend to trade at a discount to their NAVs. Since an investment fund, whether a hedge fund or a private equity fund, is a portfolio of securities, an interest in it may warrant at least a discount to NAV (irrespective of whether such a discount is actually a discount for lack of control or something else altogether).

Appraisers who do not apply a discount for lack of control to fund interests believe that the discount is not warranted for at least the following two reasons. First, control over the portfolio composition and other fund management matters—often a stated goal of an FLP—is irrelevant to a fund investor. A typical investment fund is managed professionally pursuant to a specific investment strategy/mandate, and investors invest in the fund because they believe that the manager's investment skills, experience, and incentives will result in a rate of return superior to that which the investors could earn elsewhere. Thus, although the fund investors give up control over capital that they contribute to the fund, they do so in exchange for an opportunity to earn a superior return. Second, the proponents of applying a discount for lack of control cite market evidence, namely that price-to-NAV discounts for closed-end funds are likely reflective of factors other than lack of control. For example, Nuveen, a provider of closed-end fund data widely used by appraisers, attributes divergence of closed-end funds' prices from NAV to the fact that a closed-end fund's share price is largely determined by demand and supply.[10] Fidelity pointed out several typical factors affecting demand and supply for closed-end fund shares, and the resulting divergence of the prices of closed-end funds from NAV, including:

---

10. Nuveen, "What to Know About Buying Closed-End Funds at a Discount," last modified May 23, 2025, https://www.nuveen.com/en-us/insights/closed-end-funds/what-to-know-about-buying-closed-end-funds-at-a-discount; Fidelity Investments, "Closed-End Fund (CEF) Discounts and Premiums," last visited December 14, 2025, https://www.fidelity.com/learning-center/investment-products/closed-end-funds/discounts-and-premiums.

- Distribution rates
- Market volatility
- Brand recognition of fund family and name recognition (or lack thereof) of the fund manager
- An asset class or investment strategy falling out of market favor or rising in the market's esteem

The authors' consensus is that a discount for lack of control should not be applied to direct fund interests, unless specific facts and circumstances suggest otherwise. In either case, the best practice is for an appraiser to explain the position taken, provide support for that position with references to specific documents or other evidence, and evaluate all discounts applied to NAV for reasonableness based on a resulting overall NAV reduction.

Discount for Lack of Liquidity/Marketability[11]

In the case of fund interests, a discount for lack of marketability is often considered because these interests are usually subject to restrictions on sale and transferability (or, in the case of hedge fund interests, the interests are subject to the fund's redemption policy).

Discount for Lack of Marketability for Hedge Fund Interests

Partnership interests in hedge funds are typically subject to the fund's redemption policy, which may provide for monthly, quarterly, annual, or even longer redemption windows and often requires an advance notification to the fund's GP. Thus, these interests often have a quantifiable holding period that can aid in quantifying the discount. Let's consider the following example. A hedge fund allows investors to redeem their interests from the fund at the end of each quarter; however, investors must typically provide a written notice of their intent to redeem 90 days in advance. If the investor submits a redemption notice on January 15, the investor would receive the funds only on June 30, or 166 days after submitting the notice (i.e., the 90-day notice requirement submitted on January 15 would make the investor eligible for the redemption on April 15, but since the actual redemption can occur only at the end of each quarter, the investor would have to wait until June 30). Given their quantifiable holding period, hedge fund

11. For purposes of this discussion, the terms "liquidity" and "marketability" are used interchangeably to mean an investor's ability to readily redeem or otherwise convert the fund's interest into cash.

interests are well suited for the application of option pricing models, such as protective put models, to estimate the appropriate discounts for lack of marketability.[12]

Discounts for Lack of Marketability for Private Equity Fund Interests

As we pointed out earlier in this chapter, unlike hedge fund investors, investors in private equity funds typically do not have explicit redemption/withdrawal rights and are generally restricted from transferring their interests to third parties. The most common way for such investors to exit their fund investments is to wait for the fund to sell all of its investments and to receive distributions in excess of capital contributions. Considering that private equity funds have a typical life span of at least ten years, private equity investing is usually a very long commitment. Given these interests' characteristics, the interests' values are routinely reduced by discounts for lack of marketability.

Appraisers often cite restricted stock studies among the sources of information for discounts for lack of marketability for private equity fund interests. Whatever the source of the discount data used, however, it is important to note that a discount for lack of marketability is a function of not only a holding period, but also the expected cash flow (i.e., distributions). Therefore, all else being equal, a discount for lack of marketability will vary with the stage of the fund's life cycle: the discount is normally the highest at the beginning of the fund's term (given the expected long holding period and long period before investors can start receiving distributions) and progressively declines as the fund matures (given the expected shorter holding period as the fund nears the end of its term, and consistent distributions as the fund's investments are sold off).

---

12. The essence of this approach is that since a put option provides downside protection if the value of a security, such as a share of stock or, in our case, a hedge fund interest, declines during a holding period, the value of a put option effectively represents the cost of insurance for the downside protection of value of the subject security. A discount for lack of marketability is simply a ratio of value of a put option to the value of the subject security. Obviously, the application of the protective put methodology to securities other than stocks is rather theoretical: while put options on public stocks trade on organized exchanges, puts on hedge fund interests simply do not exist. Some appraisers have also argued that a costless collar option strategy and a variable prepaid forward contract are better suited for determining a discount for lack of marketability because these strategies attempt to lock in the current value of the subject security (or in the case of a variable prepaid forward contract, typically, the concentrated portfolio), rather than to provide only a downside protection. These alternate methodologies, however, have not gained wide adoption, and they are generally subject to the same criticisms as the protective put models.

In discussing the discount for lack of marketability, it is important to address secondary transactions of LP interests, or "secondaries." In these transactions, which often involve institutional investors,[13] an investor transfers their interest to another investor who becomes an LP in the fund and assumes the transferring investor's remaining capital commitment to the fund. With the proliferation of professionally managed investment funds that specialize in these special situation transactions in recent years, a fairly robust secondaries market has emerged. In a secondary transaction, an LP interest is often transferred at a discount to NAV, which some appraisers conflate with a discount for lack of marketability. Commentary from financial intermediaries, asset management firms specializing in secondary investments, and other market participants, however, points to motivations behind such secondary transactions that have little to do with marketability. Examples of the motivations of LPs who seek to transfer their fund interests (and associated capital commitments) include asset allocation considerations[14] and cash flow/liquidity pressures,[15] to name a few. Considering these prevailing motivations, a discount to NAV that the LP interests are often transferred at may represent, in part, the cost to transfer a capital commitment (i.e., an incentive for a transferee to assume the transferring LP's remaining capital commitments to the fund), rather than an implied discount for lack of liquidity/marketability. Given the fact that the LPs' capital commitments are highest at the beginning of the private equity fund's term and decline as the fund calls capital, the observed discounts to NAV in secondary transactions tend to follow the same pattern: they are generally highest at the beginning of the fund's term and decline as the fund matures. Another important consideration when relying on secondary transaction data is that, as we pointed out earlier in this chapter, in these transactions, the transferring LPs are usually institutional investors. In divorce matters, however, appraisers and counsel often deal with interests held by a private equity firm's insiders and individual investors. These interest holders do not have access to the secondaries markets (in the case of insiders, a transfer would also likely be construed as a negative signal, i.e., a reduction in "skin in the game," to the fund's LPs or even a violation of contractual terms of the fund's partnership agreement). Therefore, when appraisers choose to

---

13. Although secondary transactions sometimes involve noninstitutional investors, data on these transactions is scarce and the transactional motivations of these investors are materially different from those of institutional investors.

14. Such considerations may be an LP's desire to reduce an overall investment portfolio's exposure to private equity as an asset class, or to reduce an allocation to a specific fund manager.

15. Cash flow/liquidity pressures arise when an LP faces a shortfall of cash to fund the remaining capital commitments, and thus chooses to transfer the interest in the secondary market rather than default on capital commitments to the investment fund.

use secondary transaction data as the basis for a discount on the value of interests held by private equity firm insiders and individual investors, they should adjust the observed discounts to NAV accordingly.

Summary

Hedge fund stakes are usually reported at fair value and investors can redeem the stakes on set dates. Private equity fund interests lack redemption rights and instead pay out over many years, so a cash flow model would be ideal to value these interests—yet outside investors rarely possess the requisite projections to use this approach, leaving appraisers to start with the reported capital account balances and make informed adjustments. While there is some divergence of practice regarding the application of a discount for lack of control for LP interests in these professionally managed investment funds, a discount for lack of marketability is generally applied. For hedge fund interests, a discount for lack of marketability is usually based on redemption terms. For private equity fund interests, the discount typically changes with the fund's life cycle. Although a robust secondary market for LP interests in private equity funds has developed, the market participants are typically institutional, not individual, investors. Therefore, when appraisers choose to use secondary transaction data as the basis for a discount on the value of interests held by private equity firm insiders and individual investors, they should consider adjusting the observed discounts to NAV accordingly.

Chapter 8

Valuation of Interests in Management Entities

As discussed in Chapter 2, management entities in both hedge funds and private equity funds are operating entities that provide investment management services to investment funds. A management entity is also the entity that is often registered as an investment adviser with the Securities and Exchange Commission,[1] or for hedge fund management firms, as a commodity pool operator with the National Futures Association. The management entity employs the firm's investment and support personnel, and it pays compensation and other operating expenses. As the investment adviser to the funds, the management entity earns management fees that are typically a percentage of assets under management (AUM) (and, in the case of private equity firms, certain other fees that may be paid directly by portfolio companies).

Value Drivers

For all asset management firms, AUM, investment performance,[2] and fee structure present three of the most important drivers of a firm's enterprise value.[3]

1. As of this book's writing, the registration threshold for management entities is at least $100 million of assets under management.

2. Here, investment performance represents the expected total gross return on AUM over a period (usually, one year) before deductions for management fees and incentive fees/carried interest. For private equity funds, the measures of investment performance are typically an internal rate of return (IRR) and a multiple of invested capital (MOIC), which represent a total return over an entire investment holding period.

3. In some jurisdictions, courts distinguish between value of an enterprise and value of personal goodwill of the enterprise owner(s). This section discusses the drivers of the firm's value in general irrespective of how value may be allocated and what it may be attributed to in a specific jurisdiction.

AUM

AUM is an important value driver because management fees are typically assessed as a percentage of AUM. For hedge funds, AUM generally represents all invested, fee-paying AUM. In private equity funds, AUM, as a concept, is more nuanced. In these types of funds, invested capital (i.e., a portion of the investors' capital commitments actually called and invested in portfolio securities) forms the basis of the fund's AUM. However, since private equity fund investors typically pay management fees as a percentage of their total capital commitments (rather than invested capital) during the fund's investment period, invested capital alone can significantly understate the management fee base, especially for newly raised funds that have significant uncalled capital commitments.

Investment Performance and Track Record

The historical performance (i.e., the investment manager's historical "track record") and the expected investment performance are two important value drivers for at least two reasons. First, superior investment returns generate incentive fees for hedge fund managers and earn carried interest distributions for private equity fund managers. Second, a manager's track record of achieving superior investment typically makes the AUM "stickier," as investors are less likely to leave a successful manager during short periods of underperformance; it also helps with attracting new capital (for hedge fund managers) and raising new funds (for private equity managers).

Valuation of Hedge Fund Management Entities

Overall Approach

The discounted cash flow (DCF) method is a frequently used (and often preferred) methodology for valuing management entities. The DCF method is based on a multi-period projection of the after-tax cash flow. In the case of a hedge fund management entity, the projected cash flow consists of (1) the expected management fees based on the AUM, (2) less the projected operating expenses. It is atypical for hedge fund managers to prepare their own projections of these components of cash flow. When these managers prepare projections, they do so usually for internal cash management purposes; therefore, the projections tend to be based on "run-rate" assumptions[4] and thus may be overly conservative, and often cover only a short period, typically no more than one year. Therefore, as a practical matter, when valuing management entities, appraisers have to develop their own projections of fees and operating expenses, starting with the forecast of the aforementioned value drivers—AUM and expected gross investment return.

AUM Forecast

The AUM forecast typically begins with the fee-paying AUM as of the valuation date. The AUM for each forecast period is determined by considering any anticipated or projected investor capital contributions and redemptions, as well as the expected gross investment return for the period. Although future capital contributions and redemptions are an important input into the AUM forecast, in the authors' experience, the expected investment return is the assumption that often causes disagreements and material divergence of value opinions between experts, and thus warrants further discussion.

We began this section with an observation that a fund manager's track record was an important value driver. All too often, however, appraisers rely solely on the fund manager's historical investment returns as a predictor of expected future returns without fully understanding the reasons behind the historical investment performance. The AUM forecast should consider the expected future investment performance based on consideration of factors such as the expected conditions of the relevant markets during the forecast period, investment strategy scalability, and the fund's historical performance relative to appropriate markets or investment strategy benchmarks or broad market indices, to name a few, in addition to an understanding of why and how the fund achieved its investment returns historically.

Length of the Forecast Period

Should the AUM forecast cover two years, five years, ten years? There are no hard-and-fast rules or rules of thumb to answer this question; the duration of the forecast period is usually dependent on the facts and circumstances of the case. It should be noted that the longer the forecast period, the more challenging it becomes to project investment performance, investors'

4. Meaning, the existing AUM and fee rates, and excluding investment performance.

behavior (i.e., contributions and redemptions), market conditions, and other variables that can affect future AUM.

Management Fee Projections

Management fees are usually projected by applying a management fee rate to an average AUM in each forecast period.[5] Figure 8.1 presents an illustration of the AUM and management fee forecast for a fund with aggregate AUM of $1,000,000, allocated between $600,000 of Class A partnership interests with an annual management fee rate of 2% and $400,000 of Class B partnership interests with an annual management fee rate of 1%. The illustration also assumes an annual gross investment return of 10% and net annual contributions of 5% of the beginning AUM for each partnership interest class in each period.

Operating Expenses

Profitability is directly correlated with a firm's value (i.e., the more profitable the firm is, the more valuable it is, all else being equal). A fund management entity is no exception. Since operating expenses directly affect a fund management entity's profitability, analysis and projections of these expenses are an important element of the valuation process. Compensation expense is typically the largest expense category for a hedge fund management entity, often accounting for as much as 60% of the management fee revenue. Reported compensation expense typically presents two issues to appraisers.

First, management entities in the United States are typically partnerships or limited liability companies. Their owners, as well as employees who participate in the firm's profits via profits interest grants, are treated as partners for U.S. income tax purposes.[6] These individuals often may only receive income in the form of partnership distributions, rather than typical

---

5. If the fund's AUM is composed of multiple partnership unit classes with varying fee structures, the management fees are calculated by applying the class-specific fee rate to that unit class's AUM. As a practical matter, the average AUM is calculated without the management fee to avoid a circular reference in the calculation.

6. Because the profits interest holders are treated as partners for U.S. income tax purposes, they receive K-1 Schedules from the management entity that report the holders' respective share of the management entity's profits, losses, and distributions. This income tax treatment of the profits interest holders confuses some appraisers and matrimonial counsel into an often mistaken conflation of the holders' tax treatment and the actual ownership of the management entity.

Figure 8.1
Illustration of the AUM and Management Fee Forecast

	Y+0	Y+1	Y+2	Y+3
Class a AUM Projection:				
Class A, BoP, [a]	A	**$ 600,000**	**$ 678,585**	**$ 767,463**
Contributions, Net of Redemptions	B	30,000	33,929	38,373
Gross Return, 10%	C	61,500	69,555	78,665
Management Fee, 2%		(12,915)	(14,607)	(16,520)
Class A, EoP, [b]	**$1,000,000**	**$ 678,585**	**$ 767,463**	**$ 867,981**
Management Fee Calculation:				
Class A, BoP		600,000	678,585	767,463
Class A, EoP Before Management Fee	=A+B+C	691,500	782,069	884,501
Average AUM (Management Fee Base)		**$ 645,750**	**$ 730,327**	**$ 825,982**
Management Fee, 2%		$ 12,915	$ 14,607	$ 16,520
Class B AUM Projection:				
Class B, BoP	A	400,000	456,695	521,426
Contributions, Net of Redemptions	B	20,000	22,835	26,071
Gross Return, 10%	C	41,000	46,811	53,446
Fees, 1%		(4,305)	(4,915)	(5,612)
Class B, EoP	**$1,000,000**	**$ 456,695**	**$ 521,426**	**$ 595,331**
Management Fee Calculation:				
Class B, BoP (Management Fee Calc)		400,000	456,695	521,426
Class B, EoP Before Management Fee	=A+B+C	461,000	526,341	600,943
Average AUM (Management Fee Base)		430,500	491,518	561,185
Management Fee, 1%		4,305	4,915	5,612
Total Project Management Fees:				
Class A Fees		$ 12,915	$ 14,607	$ 16,520
Class B Fees		4,305	4,915	5,612
Total Projected Management Fees		**$ 17,220**	**$ 19,522**	**$ 22,131**

[a] BoP: beginning of the period.

[b] EoP: end of the period.

salaries and bonuses, that are not reflected as compensation expense in the management entity's results of operations. Therefore, the reported compensation expense often requires adjustments to reflect the replacement compensation for these individuals that is subsumed in their partnership distributions.

Second, in a typical alternative asset management industry organizational structure, in which a management entity is separate from the fund's general partner entity that receives an incentive allocation,[7] the employees' performance bonuses that are tied to the earned incentive allocation are often paid by the management entity, rather than the general partner entity. The bonuses may be funded with proceeds from a redemption of the general partner interest in the fund; the bonuses are treated as capital contributions to the management entity, rather than incentive fee revenue in the management entity's results of operations. This bonus funding arrangement creates a mismatch between the reported fee revenue and compensation expense. Therefore, the compensation expense needs to be adjusted to properly align the operating expense with revenue for both the management and the general partner entities.[8]

Figure 8.2 presents an illustration of the compensation expense adjustments. In this illustration, the management entity's reported results of operations did not include any compensation for the hedge fund firm's only principal, but included $5,000 of employee bonuses, which were based on the incentive allocation that the hedge fund firm's general partner, owned by the same principal, received from the fund. The adjustments to the management entity's reported results may include (1) a recognition of the principal's replacement compensation of $1,375,[9] and (2) a removal of the employees' performance bonuses.[10]

As Figure 8.2 illustrates, the adjusted operating profit margin, a more accurate representation of the management entity's profitability, is 25.8%, compared to the reported operating profit margin of 3.1% in the example.[11]

7. A detailed discussion of typical fund management structures is presented in Chapter 5.

8. This approach is generally preferred to the alternative approach of adding the incentive fee revenue to the management entity's results of operations because it provides for a clear separation of cash flow streams with very different risk profiles (a discussion of the incentive allocation cash flow is discussed in Chapter 9).

9. As explained in footnote b to Figure 8.2, for purposes of this illustration, the principal's replacement compensation is assumed to be 25% of the management entity's adjusted operating profit before principal's compensation.

10. As will be discussed in Chapter 9, these performance-based bonuses are considered as part of the valuation analysis of the hedge fund's general partner entity.

11. While this section focuses on adjustments to compensation, typically the largest expense category, adjustments to other reported expenses may also be necessary, as is often the case in business valuation.

Figure 8.2

Illustration of the Compensation Expense Adjustments

		Reported Results	Common Size	Adjustments		Adjusted Results	Common Size
Revenue							
Management Fee, Class A	[a]	$ 12,000				$ 12,000	
Management Fee, Class B	[a]	4,000				4,000	
Total Fee Revenue		**$ 16,000**	**100.0%**			**$ 16,000**	100.0%
Operating Expenses							
Compensation:							
Principal	$ -			$ 1,375	[b]	1,375	
Employees	6,000					6,000	
Bonuses, Performance-Based	$5,000			(5,000)	[c]		
Total Compensation		11,000	68.8%			7,375	46.1%
Data, Research and Related Expenses		1,500	9.4%	–		1,500	9.4%
Occupancy		2,000	12.5%	–		2,000	12.5%
Other Operating Expenses		1,000	6.3%	–		1,000	6.3%
Total Operating Expenses		**$ 15,500**	96.9%			$ 11,875	74.2%
Operating Profit		**$ 500**	3.1%			$ 4,125	25.8%

[a] The management fees are based on the example used in Figure 8.1. The Class A management fee is calculated by applying the Class A management fee of 2% to the Class A AUM of $600,000 and the Class B management fee is calculated by applying the Class B management fee of 1% to the Class B AUM of $400,000.

[b] The adjustment to recognize the principal's replacement compensation estimated to be 25% of the adjusted operating profit before the principal's compensation.

[c] Remove performance bonuses based on the incentive allocation received by the general partner entity.

Other Considerations for Determining the Management Entity's Cash Flow

To determine the management entity's cash flow, the adjusted operating profit should be tax-affected using the appropriate tax rate.

Management entities have a straightforward business model: they receive management fees and pay compensation and other expenses necessary to run an investment advisory operation. Thus, these entities usually do not have significant working capital reserve requirements, like a traditional widget-making business may have. Nevertheless, the management fee collection patterns (i.e., monthly, quarterly, etc.) may require firms to maintain sufficient working capital to pay operating expenses between the management fee payment dates. Therefore, usually, working capital requirements may be reasonably estimated as an amount of operating expenses for the number of months corresponding to the management fee collection cycle (e.g., three months of operating expenses if the management fee is paid quarterly).

Terminal Value

Consideration of the terminal value in the valuation of a business on a going concern basis is usually not a controversial issue. For hedge fund management entities, however, the appropriateness of the terminal value, and the implicit presumption of a firm's perpetual life span, should not be the default assumption, but rather a finding that should be based on the facts and circumstances of the case.

Hedge fund management can be a fickle business. The manager's track record, while valuable, can only take the manager so far, as investors can quickly turn their backs on a fund when its investment performance falters. Unlike traditional businesses that can borrow their way through tough times, hedge fund management entities often lack assets that could be used as collateral, a typical loan requirement. In addition, managers often have a strong incentive and preference to return capital to the investors and cease operations and not borrow when the fund underperforms, to preserve their track record, rather than continuing to operate the fund hoping for a turnaround. This performance-related risk to the fund's longevity is particularly relevant to single-strategy funds that lack investment strategy diversification.

Age and intention of the hedge fund management firm's principals, and their ability and willingness to transition their duties to others within the firm, are examples of additional factors that affect consideration of the applicability of terminal value and the risk associated with it. Lack of succession planning tends to be a more prevailing issue in the hedge fund industry, due, in part, to managers' personalities, and, in part, to low exit barriers.[12]

Finally, longevity also depends on the size of the AUM, and the type and diversity of the investor base. Smaller AUM does not provide a sufficient management fee base to provide a cash flow cushion if the AUM declines due to redemptions or underperformance. Similarly, the AUM dominated by retail[13] investors usually presents a significant "AUM flight" risk as this category of investors has been shown to chase near-term performance and to be the first to abandon managers when funds underperform.

What does all this mean for a management entity's terminal value? Unless there are sufficient facts and evidence that point to the appropriateness of the terminal value (e.g., large AUM, diversified investor base, collective decision-making process at the firm, multiple portfolio managers that are responsible for meaningful portions of the firm-wide AUM, etc.), an extended cash flow forecast that covers a period over which the firm can reasonably be expected to operate may be a more practical approach. Figures 8.3 and 8.4 provide examples of the use of the terminal value and extended cash flow forecast in a valuation analysis using the illustrative management fee forecast from Figure 8.1 and adjusted operating profit margin from Figure 8.2.

As Figures 8.3 and 8.4 illustrate, the use of terminal value can have a material impact on the value of the management entity; it is one of the frequent causes of significant differences between experts.

Cost of Capital Considerations

Although all generally accepted methods for determining cost of capital, specifically cost of equity, may be used to estimate a discount rate for the hedge fund management entity's cash flow, appraisers should exercise caution when relying exclusively on the build-up method. As of the writing of this book, the only industry classification that had some relevance to hedge funds in the Kroll Cost of Capital Navigator,[14] a widely used source of cost of capital data, was Global Industry Classification Standard (GICS)

---

12. Although virtually every asset management firm touts a team approach in its investment decision-making process in the fund interest offering documents, it is important to understand the offering documents for what they are, (i.e., sales pitches to potential investors), and to review the funds' partnership agreements and other organizational documents to ascertain who the actual decision-makers ("key persons") are. Such a review is especially important for smaller asset management firms.

13. Here, "retail" means individual rather than institutional investors.

14. Cost of Capital Navigator, © 2025 Kroll, LLC. All rights reserved.

Figure 8.3
Illustrative Example with Terminal Value

	Projected				
	Y+0	Y+1	Y+2	Y+3	Terminal Value
Management Fees	$ 16,000	$ 17,220	$ 19,522	$ 22,131	
Annual Change		7.60%	13.40%	13.40%	
Adjusted Operating Margin	25.80%	25.80%	25.80%	25.80%	
Operating Profit (EBIT)	$ 4,125	$ 4,440	$ 5,033	$ 5,706	
Income Tax, 40.0%		(1,776)	(2,013)	(2,282)	
After-Tax Profit		$ 2,664	$ 3,020	$ 3,423	
Changes in Working Capital (see below)		(226)	(427)	(484)	
Net Cash Flow		**$ 2,437**	**$ 2,593**	**$ 2,593**	
Y+3 Operating Profit (EBIT)					$ 5,706
Exit Multiple				[a]	6.4x
Terminal Value					**$ 36,517**
Discounting Period (Mid-Year Convention)		0.5	1.5	2.5	3.0
Present Value Factor, 17.0%		0.9245	0.7902	0.6754	0.6244
Present Value of Cash Flow		**$ 2,253**	**$ 2,049**	**$ 1,985**	**$ 36,517**
Sum of Present Values	**$ 42,804**				
Implied Multiple of Y+0 Operating Profit (EBIT)	10.4x				
Working Capital:					
Adjusted Operating Expenses, % of Fees	74.20%	74.20%	74.20%	74.20%	
Adjusted Operating Expenses	$11,875	$12,780	$14,489	$16,426	
Management Fee Payment Frequency	4	4	4	4	
Adjusted Quarterly Expenses/Working Capital	$2,969	$3,195	$3,622	$4,106	
Working Capital, EoP		$3,195	$3,622	$4,106	
Working Capital, BoP		$2,969	$3,195	$3,622	
Projected Annual Increases in Working Capital		**$226**	**$427**	**$484**	

[a] The exit EBIT multiple implies an average net cash flow growth rate of approximately 9% after the forecast period.

[b] EoP: end of the period.

[c] BoP: beginning of the period.

Figure 8.4

Illustrative Example with Extended Cash Flow Forecast and No Terminal Value

	Base Forecast Period					Extended Forecast Period				
	Y+1	**Y+2**	**Y+3**	**Y+4**	**Y+5**	**Y+6**	**Y+7**	**Y+8**	**Y+9**	**Y+10**
Net Cash Flow, [a]	**$ 2,437**	**$ 2,593**	**$ 2,939**	**$ 3,332**	**$ 3,777**	**$ 4,282**	**$ 4,855**	**$ 5,504**	**$ 6,239**	**$ 7,073**
Net Cash Flow Growth, [b]		6.40%	13.40%							
Discounting Period (Mid-Year Convention)	0.5	1.5	2.5	3.5	4.5	5.5	6.5	7.5	8.5	9.5
Present Value Factor, 17.0%	0.9245	0.7902	0.6754	0.5772	0.4934	0.4217	0.3604	0.308	0.2633	0.225
Present Value of Cash Flow	**$ 2,253**	**$ 2,049**	**$ 1,985**	**$ 1,923**	**$ 1,864**	**$ 1,806**	**$ 1,750**	**$ 1,695**	**$ 1,643**	**$ 1,592**
Sum of Present Values	**$ 18,559**									
Implied Multiple of Y+0 Operating Proft (EBIT), [c]	4.5x									

[a] Refer to Figure 8.3 for the base forecast period net cash flow.

[b] Net cash flow is projected to grow at 13.4% annually during the extended forecast period.

[c] The Y+0 Operating Profit (EBIT) in $4,125. See Figure 8.3.

Code 40203010, Asset Management and Custody Banks. This industry classification included approximately 60 companies, ranging from bank holding and business development companies to private equity firms and hedge fund managers. Since many of this industry classification's constituent companies earn carried interest and other forms of incentive income, their risk profiles may be materially different from the risk profile of a hedge fund management entity that only earns management fee income. An adjusted capital pricing model, which usually relies on data from publicly traded management fee-only asset managers, may be a more reliable tool for determining the cost of capital for the management fee cash flow stream.

Valuation of Private Equity Management Entities

Overall Approach

Like the approach to valuing hedge fund management entities, a DCF method that is based on a multi-period projection of the after-tax cash flow is the preferred methodology for valuing private equity fund management entities. Management-prepared fee projections are more common in private equity. This is because private equity management fees tend to be more predictable compared to hedge fund management fees, especially for newly raised funds, whose investors pay management fees on their capital commitments, rather than on capital called for portfolio investments. When private equity managers prepare projections, however, they also do so usually for internal cash management purposes and for short periods (certainly for periods that are typically shorter than the remaining terms of the active investment funds). Therefore, although well-developed management forecasts are helpful, as a practical matter, appraisers often need to supplement or extend these forecasts, or when a forecast is not available, develop their own projections of management and other fees and operating expenses.

Management and Other Fee Projections

In reviewing or developing a private equity management entity's revenue projections, readers should be aware of several industry practices that can complicate the review or analysis. Private equity firms not only provide investment advisory services to their sponsored funds, but also frequently act as investment bankers and advisers to the funds' portfolio companies. For their investment banking and advisory services, private equity firms usually earn transaction, monitoring, and other advisory fees from the portfolio companies. These ancillary fees typically offset all or a portion of the management fees that private equity firms charge investors for managing the funds. A management fee waiver is another arrangement between a private equity fund's general partner and the fund's investors that can affect management fee projections and the management entity's profitability.[15]

Figure 8.5 presents an illustration of the management and other fee projections for a private equity fund with $1.1 million of commitments, of which the investors and the fund's general partner committed $1.0 million and $100,000, respectively. The fund has a term of six years, split equally between the investment period and exit period, and is expected to invest in three portfolio companies. The investors in the fund will be subject to an annual management fee of 2.5%, which, consistent with industry practices, will be calculated based on the investors' total capital commitments during the investment period and based on the investors invested capital (i.e., the amount of capital drawn down for portfolio investments) during the exit period. In this illustration, the general partner elected to waive up to $30,000 in management fees, and any ancillary fees to be earned by the manager directly from the portfolio companies in any given year of the forecast period will offset the management fee for that year by the amount equal to the lesser of (1) 80% of the ancillary fee earned or (2) the actual management fee.

Figure 8.6 summarizes the resulting utilization of the investors and general partner's commitments from the previous example.

Figure 8.7 summarizes the management entity's projected fee revenue from the investment fund in our example.

If the management entity managed more than one investment fund, as is typically the case, the same analysis and calculations would need to be applied and performed for all of the funds under management.

15. A management fee waiver is an irrevocable election by the fund's general partner to waive a portion of the management fee so that the investors' capital contributions equal to the amount of waived management fees are instead used to satisfy the general partner's capital commitment to the fund. Management fee waivers have no impact on the fund's investors' cash flow: the investors are still required to contribute capital in the amount of the management fees payable. The fund's general partners, who also typically share in the economics of the management entity and whose capital commitments to the fund are funded with the investors' contributions initially designed for management fees, get the benefit of changing the character of their income from ordinary (i.e., income that is subject to higher ordinary income taxes) to capital gains (i.e., investment income that, given the long-term nature of private equity investments, is typically taxed at long-term capital gains tax rate).

Figure 8.5

Illustrative Example of the Management and Other Fee Projections for a Private Equity Fund

	Total	% of Gross Commitments	Less: Estimated Fees, [a]	Commitments Available for Investments	% of Commitments Available for Investments
Investors' Commitments	$1,000,000	90.90%	($77,400)	$922,600	90.20%
GP's Commitments	$100,000	9.10%		100,000	9.80%
Total Fund Commitments	$1,100,000		($77,400)	$1,022,600	
Annual Management Fee	2.50%				
Amount of Management Fees Waived	30,000				
Management Fee Offset %	80.0%				
Projected MOIC at Investment Exit	2.0x				
Monitoring Annual Fee Per Investment	2,000				
Transaction Fee as % of Exit Value	3.00%				

[a] Estimated fees include management and any other projected fees during the investment period, net of management fee offsets and without reduction for the management fee waivers.

Figure 8.5

Illustrative Example of the Management and Other Fee Projections for a Private Equity Fund *(continued)*

		Investment Period				Exit Period		
	Y+0	Y+1	Y+2	Y+3	Y+4	Y+5	Y+6	Totals
Projected Fund-Level Activity:								
Commitments Avail For Investments	$ 1,022,600							
Investment Activity:								
Portfolio Investment 1		$ (340,867)			$ 681,733			
Portfolio Investment 2			$ (340,867)			$ 681,733		
Portfolio Investment 3				$ (340,867)			$ 681,733	
Total Portfolio Investments		1	2	3	2	1	0	
Management Fee Base:								
Invested Capital, EoP		$ -	$ 307,533	$ 615,067	$ 922,600	$ 615,067	$ 307,533	$ -
Additions		307,533	307,533	307,533	–	–	–	**922,600**
Exits		–	–	–	(307,533)	(307,533)	(307,533)	**(922,600)**
Invested Capital, EoP		$ 307,533	$ 615,067	$ 922,600	$ 615,067	$ 307,533	$ -	**$ -**

Figure 8.5

Illustrative Example of the Management and Other Fee Projections for a Private Equity Fund *(continued)*

Management Fee Base		Commitments	Commitments	Commitments	Invested Capital	Invested Capital	Invested Capital	
Gross Management Fee	[c]	$ 25,000	$ 25,000	$ 25,000	$ 19,221	$ 11,533	$ 3,844	**$ 109,598**
Monitoring Fees	[d]	2,000	4,000	6,000	4,000	2,000	–	**18,000**
Transaction Fees	[e]	–	–	–	20,452	20,452	20,452	**61,356**
Total Calculated Gross Fees		$ 27,000	$ 29,000	$ 31,000	$ 43,675	$ 33,985	$ 24,296	**$ 188,954**
Less Management Fee Offsets	[f]	(1,600)	(3,200)	(4,800)	(19,221)	(11,533)	(3,844)	**(44,198)**
Less Management Fee Waiver	[g]	(23,400)	(6,600)	–	–	–	–	**(30,000)**
Net Fees		2,000	19,200	26,200	24,452	22,452	20,452	**114,756**
Including:								
Net Management Fee			15,200	20,200				**35,400**
Monitoring Fees		2,000	4,000	6,000	4,000	2,000		**18,000**
Transaction Fees					20,452	20,452	20,452	**61,356**

[b] Invested capital additions represent investors' 90.2% share of the projected portfolio investment acquisition cost based on the fund's total capital commitments available for portfolio investments.

[c] Gross management fee is calculated as 2.5% of the investors' total capital commitments during the investment period and 2.5% of the average invested capital (i.e., investors' capital drawn down for portfolio investments, during the exit period).

[d] Monitoring fees are calculated by multiplying an annual monitoring fee per investment of $2,000 by the projected number of investments to be made by the fund in each year during the investment period.

[e] Transaction fees are calculated as 3.0% of the projected exit value of the investment.

[f] Management fee offsets are calculated as 80.0% of the projected monitoring and transaction fees, up to the amount of the projected management fee for the year.

[g] Management fee waivers are calculated as the lesser of the management fees, net of offsets, and the general partner's 9.8% share of the total commitments available for portfolio investments, up to $30,000 of the management fees that the general partner waived.

Figure 8.6

Illustrative Example of the Capital Commitments Funding

	Investment Period			Exit Period			
	Y+1	Y+2	Y+3	Y+4	Y+5	Y+6	Totals
Summary of Commitments Utilization							
Investors							
Portfolio Investments	$ (307,533)	$ (307,533)	$ (307,533)	During the exit period, fees are projected to be self-funded from proceeds of sales of portfolio investments: thus, no contributions will be needed.			$ (922,600)
Fees	(2,000)	(19,200)	(26,200)				(47,400)
Contributions of Waived Management Fees	(23,400)	(6,600)	–				(30,000)
Total Utilized Investors' Commitments	$ (332,933)	$ (333,333)	$ (333,733)				$ (1,000,000)
General Partner							
Cash Contributions	$ (9,933)	$ (26,733)	$ (33,333)				$ (70,000)
Deemed Contributions (Waived Management Fees)	(23,400)	(6,600)	–				(30,000)
Total Utilized GP's Commitments	$ (33,333)	$ (33,333)	$ (33,333)				$ (100,000)

Figure 8.7

Illustrative Example of Management Entity's Fee Revenue Projections

	Investment Period			Exit Period			
	Y+1	Y+2	Y+3	Y+4	Y+5	Y+6	Totals
Management Fee, Net	$ -	$ 15,200	$ 20,200	$ -	$ -		**$ 35,400**
Monitoring Fees	2,000	4,000	6,000	4,000	2,000		**18,000**
Transaction Fees	–	–	–	20,452	20,452	20,452	**61,356**
Total Projected Fees	**$ 2,000**	**$ 19,200**	**$ 26,200**	**$ 24,452**	**$ 22,452**	**$ 20,452**	**$ 114,756**

Operating Expenses

The cost structure of a private equity management entity is typically similar to that of a hedge fund management entity, and the compensation issues that often require normalization adjustments tend to mirror those that we pointed out for hedge fund management entities. Therefore, we suggest that readers review the discussion of the operating expenses and related issues for the hedge fund management entities presented earlier in this chapter.

Terminal Value

The terminal value in the valuation of a private equity management entity often presents issues similar to those that we covered in our discussion of hedge fund management entity valuation earlier in this chapter, and causes significant divergence of opinions among experts, especially in matrimonial matters.

The proponents of using an ongoing terminal value in the DCF method believe that a management entity will continue as going concern, providing professional services (i.e., investment advice) to the investment funds under the private equity firm's management. Therefore, they believe the terminal value may be appropriate, and in fact a management entity should be valued on a going concern basis, except when facts and circumstances suggest a different premise.[16]

However, the issues regarding terminal value specifically, and the appropriate premise of value for a management entity generally, are more nuanced. The management entity is usually not a standalone business—it is a part of the private equity firm business/investment complex that includes a management entity, one or more general partner entities, and investment funds.[17] As an investment adviser, the management entity has no standalone value without the requisite investment funds.[18] This means that when the goal of the valuation is a determination of the private equity firm's enterprise value, the approach and assumptions for the valuation of the management entity, including whether or not the management entity should be valued on a going concern premise and thus warrant the use of a terminal value, is based on the presumption of the management entity's

16. An example of such circumstance would be if a private equity firm was no longer raising new funds.

17. For a detailed discussion of organizational structures, readers can review Chapter 5.

18. Considering the management entity in isolation from the general partner/carried interest entities and investment funds may be akin to an attempt to bifurcate a bank's deposit-taking and lending operations, even though one side of operations does not exist without the other.

continued operation, which implies that the private equity firm will continue raising new funds after the relevant valuation date. To many appraisers, the raising of new funds is too speculative and may not be included in the valuation.[19] The applicability of each treatment of the forecast period and terminal value will depend on the facts and circumstances surrounding the particular valuation assignment.

Cost of Capital Considerations

From the cost of capital determination perspective, the considerations outlined for hedge fund management entities earlier in this chapter are also relevant for private equity management entities. A determination of the cost of capital for a private equity management entity may have an additional level of complexity, however, especially if data on publicly traded private equity management firms is used. The additional complexity stems from accounting consolidation rules and their effect on a company's reported consolidated financial leverage. Per current accounting principles, asset management firms that sponsor and act as a general partner to investment funds are generally required to consolidate the funds and report the funds' assets and liabilities on the firms' consolidated balance sheets. Thus, if a firm consolidates a fund that uses a leveraged investment strategy, such as credit, the fund-level debt would be reflected on the firm's consolidated balance sheet and, if not adjusted, can result in the wrong cost of capital conclusion in some circumstances.

Summary

Valuing hedge fund and private equity management entities centers on forecasting fee-based cash flows, accurately adjusting expenses, and assessing long-term viability (including terminal value assumptions). Key inputs include AUM, investment performance, compensation normalization, fee offsets, management waivers, and investor behavior. Fund management entities also often present unique cost of capital analysis challenges, such as finding truly comparable companies, adjusting for differences in risk between fee-based and incentive-based revenues, and properly interpreting public company data.

---

19. This assumes no new funds have been started during the period prior to the valuation date.

Chapter 9

Valuation of General Partner (Special Profit Allocation) Entities

As discussed in Chapter 3, the economics of the alternative investment management business typically include not only management and other advisory fees, but also a share of the fund's investment profits (i.e., incentive fees for hedge funds and carried interest for private equity funds) and a capital component (i.e., an investment in the fund, which is usually perceived as a manager's "skin in the game"). The capital component and carried interest are usually structured as a general partner interest in the investment fund, although alternative structures are also used in which the carried interest entitlement is assigned to a special performance allocation entity.[1]

Valuation of Hedge Fund General Partner Entities

Overall Approach

Hedge fund general partner entities have the same value drivers as the affiliated management entities that were discussed in Chapter 8 (i.e., the assets under management (AUM) and expected gross investment return). Therefore, the same AUM, expected gross investment return, and fee structure assumptions that are used for valuing the management entity should be used in the valuation of the general partner entity. In fact, the same AUM forecast used for valuing the management entity should also be used to value the general partner entity.

1. Other than bifurcating the cash flows related to the capital component and carried interest, alternative structures generally have no impact on valuation approaches; therefore, alternative structures will not be covered separately in this chapter.

Performance Allocation Forecast

To illustrate the analysis, we will re-use the illustrative example presented in the Valuation of Hedge Fund Management Entities section in Chapter 8. As readers may recall, in that example, we examined a fund with aggregate AUM of $1,000,000, allocated between $600,000 of Class A partnership interests with an annual management fee rate of 2% and $400,000 of Class B partnership interests with an annual management fee rate of 1%. The example also assumed an annual gross investment return of 10% and net annual contributions of 5% of the beginning AUM for each partnership interest class in each three-year forecast period. In addition to these original fund assumptions, for purposes of this illustration we will assume that the fund's general partner entity is entitled to a performance allocation on the projected investment return, net of management fees, of 15% for Class A interests and 25% for Class B interests. Figure 9.1 illustrates the analysis of the projected performance allocation.

Operating Expenses

Hedge fund general partner entities typically do not incur material operating expenses. However, the projected performance allocation should be reduced by the projected amounts of performance-based compensation for the hedge fund manager's employees and performance-based replacement compensation for the firm's principals.[2] Finally, the resulting projected operating profit should be reduced by income taxes calculated using the appropriate income tax rate or rates.[3] Figure 9.2 summarizes the forecast of the performance allocation-related cash flow based on the performance allocation projection from Figure 9.1 and assuming a total performance-based and replacement compensation of 50% of the projected performance allocation and an income tax rate of 30%.[4]

2. A discussion of replacement compensation is presented in Chapter 8.

3. Considering that, generally, the performance allocation represents a re-allocation of investment income, including capital gains, from the fund's limited partners to the general partner, the income tax rate should reflect the nature of the allocated income. Typically, the tax rate would represent a combination of the ordinary and long-term capital gains tax rates, depending on the fund's investment strategy and trading activity. See Chapter 13 for a discussion of the relevant tax issues.

4. Because the general partner entities do not have material operating expenses, they typically do not have working capital requirements/reserves.

Figure 9.1
Illustrative Analysis of the Projected Performance Allocation

	Y+0	Y+1	Y+2	Y+3		Y+1	Y+2	Y+3
Class A AUM Projection:								
Class A, BoP	A	**$600,000**	**$671,297**	**$751,067**	**Class A, BoP**	**$600,000**	**$671,297**	**$751,067**
Contributions, Net of Redemptions	B	30,000	33,565	37,553	Contributions, Net of Redemptions	30,000	33,565	37,553
Gross Return, 10%	C	61,500	68,808	76,984	Gross Return, 10%	61,500	68,808	76,984
Management Fee, 2%		(12,915)	(14,450)	(16,167)	Management Fee, 2%	(12,915)	(14,450)	(16,167)
Class A, Before Performance Allocation	**$1,000,000**	**$678,585**	**$759,220**	**$849,438**	**Return, Net of Management Fee**	**$48,585**	**$54,358**	**$60,818**
Performance Allocation 15%		(7,288)	(8,154)	(9,123)	**Performance Allocation, 15%**	**$7,288**	**$8,154**	**$9,123**
Class A, EoP		**$671,297**	**$751,067**	**$840,315**				
Management Fee Calculation:								
Class A, BoP		600,000	671,297	751,067				
Class A, EoP Before Management Fee and Performance Allocation	=A+B+C	691,500	773,670	865,604				
Average AUM (Management Fee Base)		**$645,750**	**$722,484**	**$808,335**				
Management Fee, 2%		$12,915	$14,450	$16,167				
Class B AUM Projection:								
Class B, BoP	A	400,000	447,521	500,688	**Class B, BoP**	**$400,000**	**$447,521**	**$500,688**
Contributions, Net of Redemptions	B	20,000	22,376	25,034	Contributions, Net of Redemptions	20,000	22,376	25,034

Figure 9.1
Illustrative Analysis of the Projected Performance Allocation *(continued)*

	Y+0	Y+1	Y+2	Y+3		Y+1	Y+2	Y+3
Gross Return, 10%	C	41,000	45,871	51,321	Gross Return, 10%	41,000	45,871	51,321
Management Fee, 1%		(4,305)	(4,816)	(5,389)	Management Fee, 1%	(4,305)	(4,816)	(5,389)
Class B, Before Performance Allocation	**$1,000,000**	**$456,695**	**$510,952**	**$571,654**	**Return, Net of Management Fee**	**$36,695**	**$41,054**	**$45,932**
Performance Allocation 25%		(9,174)	(10,264)	(11,483)	**Performance Allocation, 25%**	**$9,174**	**$10,264**	**$11,483**
Class B, EoP		**$447,521**	**$500,688**	**$560,171**				
Management Fee Calculation:								
Class B, BoP		$400,000	$447,521	$500,688				
Class A, EoP Before Management Fee and Performance Allocation	=A+B+C	461,000	515,768	577,043				
Average AUM (Management Fee Base)		$430,500	$481,645	$538,866				
Management Fee, 1%		$4,305	$4,816	$5,389				
Total Projected Performance Allocation:								
Class A		$7,288	$8,154	$9,123				
Class B		9,174	10,264	11,483				
Total Projected Performance Allocation		**$16,462**	**$18,417**	**$20,606**				

Figure 9.2
Illustrative Summary of Projected Performance Allocation-Related Cash Flow

	Y+1	Y+2	Y+3
Projected Performance Allocation, Class A	$ 7,288	$ 8,154	$ 9,123
Projected Performance Allocation, Class B	9,174	10,264	11,483
Total Projected Performance Allocation	**$ 16,462**	**$ 18,417**	**$ 20,606**
Less: Performance-Based and Replacement Compensation, 50%	(8,231)	(9,209)	(10,303)
Operating Profit	**$ 8,231**	**$ 9,209**	**$ 10,303**
Less: Income Tax, 30%	(2,469)	(2,763)	(3,091)
After-Tax Cash Flow	**$ 5,762**	**$ 6,446**	**$ 7,212**

Cost of Capital Considerations

Required rates of return for the performance allocation are generally not directly observable in the marketplace; to the authors' knowledge, there were no publicly traded incentive fee-only hedge fund managers as of the writing of this book. However, rates of return could be inferred by comparing the trading multiples and required rates of return for traditional, management fee-only asset managers and publicly traded alternative asset management firms. As a rule of thumb, given their greater risk,[5] compared to management fees, the performance allocation/incentive fees are usually ascribed valuation multiples that are considerably lower than that of the management fee multiples. Let's examine the application of this rule of thumb using the information from Figures 9.1 and 9.2. Figure 9.3 illustrates a valuation of the management entity using the discounted cash flow method. In this example, we assume that the appropriate discount rate for the management fee cash flow is 17%, a terminal value is warranted, and the sustainable cash flow growth rate is 7%, based on a combination of the expected capital inflows and AUM appreciation.

5. Considering the fact that the incentive allocation is earned only when the fund achieves a positive investment return in excess of management fees, the risk can be expressed as the uncertainty of achieving the projected gross investment return. The management fee is earned regardless of the investment performance; therefore, the management fee is not subject to investment performance risk.

Figure 9.3

Illustrative Valuation of a Hedge Fund Management Entity

		Y+1	Y+2	Y+3	Terminal
Projected Management Fees					
Class A		$ 12,915	$ 14,450	$ 16,167	
Class B		4,305	4,816	5,389	
Total Projected Management Fees		**$ 17,220**	**$ 19,266**	**$ 21,555**	
Assumed Operating Profit Margin		25.8%	25.8%	25.8%	
Operating Profit (EBITDA)		$ 4,443	$ 4,971	$ 5,561	
Income Tax, 40%		(1,777)	(1,988)	(2,225)	
After-Tax Cash Flow		**$ 2,666**	**$ 2,982**	**$ 3,337**	
Changes in Working Capital	[a]	(226)	(380)	(425)	
Net Cash Flow		**$ 2,439**	**$ 2,603**	**$ 2,912**	
Projected Cash Flow Growth, Year-over-Year			6.7%	11.9%	7.0%
Terminal Cash Flow	[b]				**$ 3,290**
Capitalization Rate	[c]				10.0%
Terminal Value					**$ 32,904**
Implied Y+3 EBITDA Exit Multiple					5.9x
Net Cash Flow		$ 2,439	$ 2,603	$ 2,912	$ -
Terminal Value		–	–	–	32,904
Total Cash Flow		**$ 2,439**	**$ 2,603**	**$ 2,912**	**$ 32,904**
Discounting Period	[d]	0.5000	1.5000	2.5000	3.0000
Present Value Factors at 17%		0.9245	0.7902	0.6754	0.6244
Present Values		**$ 2,255**	**$ 2,057**	**$ 1,967**	**$ 20,545**
Sum of Present Values		**$ 26,923**			
Implied Y+1 Net Cash Flow Multiple		11.0x			
Implied Y+1 Operating Profit (EBITDA) Multiple		6.0x			

As Figure 9.3 illustrates, the indicated value of the management fee implies a cash flow multiple of 11.0 and a forward EBITDA (earnings before interest, taxes, depreciation, and amortization) (i.e., operating profit, multiple of 6.0). The rule of thumb that we described earlier suggests that, applying the same growth assumptions, the performance allocation should be valued on a cash flow multiple of approximately 5.5, or one-half of the management entity's implied net cash flow multiple. We can use this estimate to set up a discounted cash flow analysis of the performance allocation and backsolve for the discount rate that would result in the target cash flow multiple. Figure 9.4 presents the calculations.[6]

As Figure 9.4 illustrates, the discount rate that results in the performance allocation's cash flow multiple being approximately one-half of the management fee cash flow multiple is 26%.[7]

A Note on Discounting Conventions

Readers have undoubtedly noticed that the illustrations of valuation calculations for the management entities in Chapter 8 utilized a mid-year discounting convention (i.e., an assumption that the cash flow occurs evenly throughout the year). A typical pattern of hedge fund performance allocation cash flow, however, differs materially from the pattern of management fee collections. A fund's investment performance is usually measured once a year (or whenever an investor redeems their interest), and the performance allocation is finalized in the following year, after the fund's financial statement audit is completed and its performance for the measurement year is independently verified. Since it usually takes at least a couple of months after the end of the year for the financial statement audit and performance verification to be completed, a valuation analysis performed at the end of Year 0 should consider the fact the performance allocation cash flow for Year 1 is likely not going to occur until two or three months into Year 2 (i.e., approximately 14–15 months after the valuation date). This pattern of cash flow is reflected in the discounting periods used in the illustration in Figure 9.4.

---

6. "Backsolve" means an application of an iterative process to determine a discount rate, which, when used in the discounted cash flow analysis, results in the value that implies a cash flow multiple of 5.5.

7. This framework can also be used to check an independently determined performance allocation discount rate for reasonableness.

Figure 9.4

Illustrative Example of Performance Allocation Discount Rate Analysis

		Y+1	Y+2	Y+3	Terminal
Projected Performance Allocation, Class A		$7,288	$8,154	$9,222	
Projected Performance Allocation, Class B		9,174	10,264	11,483	
Total Projected Performance Allocation		**$ 16,462**	**$ 18,417**	**$ 20,606**	
Less: Performance-Based and Replacement Compensation, 50%		(8,231)	(9,209)	(10,303)	
Operating Profit		**$ 8,231**	**$ 9,209**	**$ 10,303**	
Less: Income Tax, 30%		(2,469)	(2,763)	(3,091)	
After-Tax Cash Flow		**$ 5,762**	**$ 6,446**	**$ 7,212**	
Projected Cash Flow Growth, Year-over-Year			*11.9%*	*11.9%*	*7.0%*
Terminal Cash Flow	[a]				**$ 7,717**
Capitalization Rate	[b]				18.8%
Terminal Value					**$ 41,083**
Implied Y+3 EBITDA Exit Multiple					4.0x
After-Tax Cash Flow		**$ 5,762**	**$ 6,446**	**$ 7,212**	
Terminal Value		–	–	41,083	
Total Cash Flow		**$ 5,762**	**$ 6,446**	**$ 48,295**	
Discounting Period	[c]	1.1667	2.1667	3.1667	
Present Value Factors at 26% (Implied)	[d]	0.7652	0.6083	0.4836	
Present Values		**$ 4,409**	**$ 3,921**	**$ 23,357**	
Sum of Present Values		**$ 31,688**			
Implied Y+1 Cash Flow Multiple		5.5x			
Implied Y+1 Operating Profit (EBITDA) Multiple		3.8x			

[a] The terminal cash flow is estimated as Y+3 projected fee revenue × (1 + 7% terminal growth rate) × 50.0% profit margin × (1 - 30% tax rate). The subject general partner/profit allocation entity is presumed not to have working capital reserve requirements.

[b] Based on the implied performance allocation discount rate of approximately 26%.

[c] Discounting periods are calculated using the year-end discounting convention because performance allocation is typically finalized in the year after the investment performance measurement year upon completion of the audit of the investment funds.

[d] Represents a discount rate, calculated using the backsolve, that results in the implied cash flow multiple of value to be approximately a half of the management fee cash flow multiple.

Valuation of Private Equity Fund General Partner Entities

Overall Approach

Participation of the general partners in investment activities of hedge fund and private equity funds is similar: general partners in both types of funds invest alongside funds' limited partners and receive a share of the limited partners' investment profits in the form of performance allocation/carried interest as a return on the general partners' "sweat equity" in the funds' capital appreciation. Thus, the analysis of the general partner entity's cash flow should start at the investment fund level and generally be based on the assumptions and methodologies consistent with those used in the valuation of the management entity.

To illustrate a valuation analysis of the private equity fund general partner entity, we will use the same hypothetical private equity fund that we introduced in Chapter 8 in our discussion of the valuation of the private equity fund management entity. This private equity fund has $1.1 million in commitments, of which the investors and the fund's general partner committed $1.0 million and $100,000, respectively. The fund has a term of six years, split equally between the investment period and exit period, and is expected to invest in three portfolio companies. The fund's other terms, such as the management fee, management fee offsets, and the portion of management fees that the general partner of the fund has elected to waive, are described in Chapter 8. For purposes of this illustration, an additional assumption is that the private equity fund's general partner is entitled to a 20% share of the limited partners' profits once the limited partners earn a 1.5 multiple on their capital contributed for portfolio investments, fees, and expenses.

Figure 9.5 illustrates an analysis of the general partner's cash flow using a common version of the European portfolio proceeds allocation waterfall.[8]

As Figure 9.5 illustrates, in our example of a private equity fund with a European portfolio proceeds allocation, the general partner would receive a carried interest distribution of $63,309 in Y+6. Figure 9.6 summarizes the general partner's total cash flow from the fund.

Figure 9.7 illustrates an analysis of the general partner's cash flow using an American (i.e., deal-by-deal) portfolio proceeds allocation waterfall.[9]

---

8. For the descriptions of the types of the proceeds allocation waterfalls, refer to Appendix A.

9. For ease of the illustration, we assume that the capital that is returned on a sale of a portfolio investment is the capital invested in that portfolio investment. All fees and expenses are assumed to be returned when the last investment is sold. In practice, the fees and expenses that are returned upon a sale of the portfolio investment are usually those

Figure 9.8 summarizes the general partner's total cash flow from the fund under the American style waterfall allocation scenario.

A comparison of the general partner's total cash flow under the European waterfall summarized in Figure 9.6 and the American waterfall presented in Figure 9.8 shows that, in our examples, the general partner's aggregate cash flow is the same in both scenarios, but the carried interest proceeds are realized quicker under the American waterfall.[10] Figure 9.9 illustrates a calculation of value of the general partner entity using the European waterfall cash flow from Figure 9.6.

Cost of Capital Considerations

In the valuation of private equity fund general partner entities, the same cost of capital considerations that we described for the hedge fund general partner entities earlier in this chapter also apply. When dealing with private equity funds, however, another relevant factor to consider is the fund's projected gross internal rate of return (IRR) and the achieved gross IRRs of the subject private equity firm's older funds. With a proper analysis of the differences in achieved gross IRRs across vintage years for older funds, the historical holding period returns may provide an insight into (or a reasonableness test for) a discount rate for the capital commitment component of the general partner entity. For example, in Figure 9.9, the present value of the net cash flow related to the general partner's capital commitment was calculated using a discount rate of 26%, which represents the fund's projected gross IRR.[11]

The carried interest represents a subordinated claim on the fund's cash flow because it is contingent on the fund returning capital and providing a minimum rate of return to the investors (in our simplified example, that return is a 1.5 multiple of the investors' capital invested in the portfolio companies). Therefore, arguably, a discount rate for the carried interest should be higher than the fund's projected IRR. In the present value calculation in Figure 9.9, we assumed a discount rate of 35% for the carried interest. As a reasonableness test, we can point out that the assumed discount rate is higher than the fund's projected IRR and approximately twice the base management fee discount rate that we discussed in Chapter 8.

---

specific to that investment or a pro rata share of the fees and expenses calculated as a ratio of capital invested in the sold portfolio investment to the fund's total invested capital. These terms are typically provided in the fund's limited partnership agreement.

10. The American waterfall may present a clawback risk if the investors fail to achieve a 1.5x multiple on their invested capital.

11. The projected IRR was estimated using the IRR function in Microsoft Excel. Because the IRR is time-sensitive, in practice, the IRR is calculated using the XIRR function and actual dates for the fund's historical cash flow when such historical cash flow information is available.

Figure 9.5
Illustrative Example of Private Equity Fund's General Partner's Cash Flow (European Waterfall)

		Investment Period			Exit Period			
	Y+0	**Y+1**	**Y+2**	**Y+3**	**Y+4**	**Y+5**	**Y+6**	**Totals**
Projected Fund-Level Activity:								
Commitments Avail for Investments	$ 1,022,600							
Investment Activity:								
Portfolio Investment 1		$ (340,867)			$ 681,733			
Portfolio Investment 2			$ (340,867)			$ 681,733		
Portfolio Investment 3				$ (340,867)			$ 681,733	
Total Portfolio Investments		1	2	3	2	1	–	
Investors' Share of Portfolio Proceeds		**$ -**	**$ -**	**$ -**	**$ 615,067**	**$ 615,067**	**$ 615,067**	**$ 1,845,200**
Less Expenses		–	–	–	(24,452)	(22,452)	(20,452)	**(67,356)**
Investors' Share of Portfolio Proceeds, Net		$ -	$ -	$ -	$ 590,615	$ 592,615	$ 594,615	$ 1,777,844
Allocation of Investors' Share of Proceeds:								
Return of Contributed Capital, Including								
Invested Capital		–	–	–	544,901	377,699	–	**$ 922,600**
Fees, Expenses, and Management Waivers		–	–	–	45,714	31,686	–	**$ 77,400**
Total Return of Capital		–	–	–	590,615	409,385	--	**1,000,000**
Remaining Proceeds		–	–	–	-	183,229	594,615	**777,844**
Amount Necessary to Provide 1.5x on Invested Capital					-	183,229	278,071	**$ 461,300**
Remaining Proceeds						-	316,544	**316,544**
Residual Allocation, Including								
Investors, 80.0%						-	253,235	**$ 253,235**
General Partner, 20.0% (Carried Interest)						-	63,309	**$ 63,309**

Figure 9.5
Illustrative Example of Private Equity Fund's General Partner's Cash Flow (European Waterfall) *(continued)*

		Investment Period			Exit Period			
	Y+0	**Y+1**	**Y+2**	**Y+3**	**Y+4**	**Y+5**	**Y+6**	**Totals**
Total Allocated Investors' Proceeds					590,615	592,615	594,615	**1,777,844**
Investors' Commitments Utilization:								
Portfolio Investments								
Invested Capital, BoP		$ -	$ 307,533	$ 615,067	$ 922,600	$ 377,699	$ -	**$ -**
Additions		307,533	307,533	307,533	–	–	–	**922,600**
Exits		–	–	–	(544,901)	(377,699)	–	**(922,600)**
Invested Capital, EoP		**$ 307,533**	**$ 615,067**	**$ 922,600**	**$ 377,699**			
Fees and Expenses								
Balance, BoP		$ -	$ 25,000	$ 51,000	$ 77,400	$ 31,686	$ -	**$ -**
Contributions for Fees and Expenses		2,000	19,200	26,200	–	–		**47,400**
Contributions of Waived Management Fees		23,400	6,600	–	–	–		**30,000**
Exits		–	–	–	(45,714)	(31,686)		**(77,400)**
Balance, EoP		**$ 25,400**	**$ 51,200**	**$ 77,400**	**$ 31,686**	**$ -**	**$ -**	**$ -**
Total Contributed Capital								
Balance, BoP		$ -	$ 332,933	$ 666,267	$ 1,000,000	$ 409,385	$ -	**$ -**
Contributions		332,933	333,333	333,733	–	–	–	**1,000,000**
Exits		–	–	–	(590,615)	(409,385)	–	**(1,000,000)**
Balance, EoP		**$ 332,933**	**$ 666,267**	**$ 1,000,000**	**$ 409,385**	**$ -**	**$ -**	**$ -**
BoP: beginning of period								
EoP: end of period								

Figure 9.6
Illustrative Summary of General Partner's Total Cash Flow from Private Equity Fund (European Waterfall)

		Investment Period			Exit Period			
	Y+0	Y+1	Y+2	Y+3	Y+4	Y+5	Y+6	Totals
General Partner Cash Flow:								
Cash Capital Contributions		$ (9,933)	$ (26,733)	$ (33,333)	$ -	$ -	$ -	$ (70,000)
Portfolio Proceeds, Pro Rata		–	–	–	66,667	66,667	66,667	200,000
Carried Interest		–	–	–	–	–	63,309	63,309
Total General Partner Cash Flow		**$ (9,933)**	**$ 26,733**	**$ (33,333)**	**$ 67,667**	**$ 67,667**	**$ 129,975**	**$ 193,309**

Figure 9.7
Illustrative Example of Private Equity Fund's General Partner's Cash Flow (American Waterfall)

		Investment Period			Exit Period			
	Y+0	Y+1	Y+2	Y+3	Y+4	Y+5	Y+6	Totals
Projected Fund-Level Activity:								
Commitments Avail for Investments	$1,022,600							
Investment Activity:								
Portfolio Investment 1		$(340,867)			$681,733			
Portfolio Investment 2			$(340,867)			$681,733		
Portfolio Investment 3				$(340,867)			$681,733	
Total Portfolio Investments		1	2	3	2	1	–	
Investor's Share of Portfolio Proceeds		**$ -**	**$ -**	**$ -**	**$615,067**	**$615,067**	**$615,067**	**$1,845,200**

Figure 9.7

Illustrative Example of Private Equity Fund's General Partner's Cash Flow (American Waterfall) *(continued)*

	Investment Period				Exit Period			
	Y+0	**Y+1**	**Y+2**	**Y+3**	**Y+4**	**Y+5**	**Y+6**	**Totals**
Less Expenses		–	–	–	(24,452)	(22,452)	(20,452)	**(67,356)**
Investor's Share of Portfolio Proceeds, Net		**$ -**	**$ -**	**$ -**	**$590,615**	**$592,615**	**$594,615**	**$1,777,844**
Allocation of Investors' Share of Proceeds:								
Return of Contributed Capital, Including								
Invested Capital		–	–	–	307,533	307,533	307,533	**$922,600**
Fees, Expenses, and Management Waivers		–	–	–	–	–	77,400	**$77,400**
Total Return of Capital		–	–	–	307,533	307,533	384,933	**1,000,000**
Remaining Proceeds		–	–	–	283,081	285,081	209,681	**777,840**
Amount Necessary to Provide 1.5x on Invested Capital		–	–	–	153,767	153,767	153,767	**$461,300**
Remaining Proceeds		–	–	–	129,315	131,315	55,915	**316,544**
Residual Allocation, Including								
Investors, 80.0%		–	–	–	103,452	105,052	44,732	**$253,235**
General Partner, 20.0% (Carried Interest)		–	–	–	25,863	26,263	11,183	**$63,309**
Total Allocated Investors' Proceeds		–	–	–	590,615	592,615	594,615	**1,777,844**

Figure 9.7
Illustrative Example of Private Equity Fund's General Partner's Cash Flow (American Waterfall) *(continued)*

		Investment Period			Exit Period			
	Y+0	**Y+1**	**Y+2**	**Y+3**	**Y+4**	**Y+5**	**Y+6**	**Totals**
Investors' Commitments Utilization:								
Portfolio Investments								
Invested Capital, BoP		$ -	$307,533	$615,067	$922,600	$615,067	$307,533	**$ -**
Additions		307,533	307,533	307,533	–	–	–	**922,600**
Exits		–	–	–	(307,533)	(307,533)	(307,533)	**(922,600)**
Invested Capital, EoP		**$307,533**	**$615,067**	**$922,600**	**$615,067**	**$307,533**	**$ -**	**$ -**
Fees and Expenses								
Balance, BoP		$ -	$25,000	$51,000	$77,400	$77,400	$77,400	**$ -**
Contributions for Fees and Expenses		2,000	19,200	26,200	–	–	–	**47,400**
Contributions of Waived Management Fees		23,400	6,600	–	–	–	–	**30,000**
Exits		–	–	–	–	–	(77,400)	**(77,400)**
Balance, EoP		$25,400	$51,200	$77,400	$77,400	$77,400	$ -	**$ -**
Total Contributed Capital								
Balance, BoP		$ -	$332,933	$666,267	$1,000,000	$692,467	$384,933	**$ -**
Contributions		332,933	333,333	333,733	–	–	–	**1,000,000**
Exits		–	–	–	307,533	307,533	384,933	**(1,000,000)**
Balance, EoP		**$332,933**	**$666,267**	**$1,000,000**	**$692,467**	**$384,933**	**$ -**	**$ -**

BoP: beginning of period
EoP: end of period

Figure 9.8

Illustrative Summary of General Partner's Total Cash Flow from Private Equity Fund (American Waterfall)

	Investment Period				Exit Period			
	Y+0	Y+1	Y+2	Y+3	Y+4	Y+5	Y+6	Totals
General Partner Cash Flow:								
Cash Capital Contributions		$ (9,933)	$ (26,733)	$ (33,333)	$ -	$ -	$ -	$ (70,000)
Portfolio Proceeds, Pro Rata		–	–	–	66,667	66,667	66,667	200,000
Carried Interest		–	–	–	25,863	26,263	11,183	63,309
Total General Partner Cash Flow		**$ (9,933)**	**$ 26,733**	**$ (33,333)**	**$ 92,530**	**$ 92,930**	**$ 77,850**	**$ 193,309**

Figure 9.9

Illustrative Valuation of the Private Equity Fund's General Partner Entity (European Waterfall)

	Y+0	Y+1	Y+2	Y+3	Y+4	Y+5	Y+6	Totals
Valuation of the General Partner Capital Commitment:								
Cash Capital Contributions		$(9,933)	$(26,733)	$(33,333)	$ -	$ -	$ -	**$(70,000)**
Portfolio Proceeds, Pro Rata		–	–	–	66,667	66,667	66,667	**200,000**
Pretax Cash Flow		$(9,933)	$(26,733)	$(33,333)	$66,667	$66,667	$66,667	**$130,000**
Less Income Tax	See below	0	–	–	–	(15,073)	(15,867)	**(30,940)**
After-Tax Cash Flow		**$(9,933)**	**$(26,733)**	**$(33,333)**	**$66,667**	**$51,593**	**$50,800**	**$99,060**
Net Present Value at 26.0%	[a]	$14,016	A					

Figure 9.9

Illustrative Valuation of the Private Equity Fund's General Partner Entity (European Waterfall) *(continued)*

		Y+0	Y+1	Y+2	Y+3	Y+4	Y+5	Y+6	Totals
Income Tax Calculation									
Portfolio Proceeds, Pro Rata			$ -	$ -	$ -	$66,667	$66,667	$66,667	**$200,000**
Cost Basis			–	–	–	66,667	3,333	–	**70,000**
Taxable Gain			–	–	–	–	63,333	66,667	**130,000**
Income Tax, 23.8%	[b]		–	–	–	–	15,073	15,867	**30,940**
Valuation of Carried Interest									
Projected Carried Interest Distributions			$ -	$ -	$ -	$ -	$ -	$63,309	**$63,309**
Less Income Tax, 23.8%	[b]		–	–	–	–	–	(15,067)	**(15,067)**
After-Tax Cash Flow			**$ -**	**$ -**	**$ -**	**$ -**	**$ -**	**$48,241**	**$48,241**
Net Present Value at 35.0%	[c]		$7,969	**B**					
TOTAL VALUE			$21,985	=A+B					

[a] Net present value is calculated using the fund's projected gross internal rate of return (IRR) as a discount rate for the general partner capital commitment.

[b] A long-term capital gains treatment of the proceeds is assumed. The income tax rate represents the federal long-term capital gains tax rate plus a 3.8% net investment income surcharge. The taxable proceeds may also be subject to state and local income taxes, as appropriate.

[c] A 35.0% discount rate is assumed for the carried interest cash flow.

We should caution readers, however, that the previous analysis would be appropriate for a newly launched private equity fund. Valuation considerations may be different if the fund is at a different point in its life cycle as of the valuation date. For example, if a valuation of a general partner entity is performed when the fund is in the middle of the exit period, an argument can usually be made that some aspects of the performance uncertainty that existed when the fund was launched are no longer present. Therefore, it may be possible to show that the appropriate discount rates for the components of the general partner's share in the fund may be substantially lower than they would have been at the time of the fund's launch.

Summary

In summary, valuation of a general partner entity typically involves valuation of both a capital component and carried interest. The value drivers for the general partner entity are similar to those for the management entity—they are AUM and expected gross investment return. Although the general partner entities typically do not incur material operating expenses, in valuations for matrimonial litigation purposes, the projected incentive allocation/performance fee/carried interest distributions should be reduced by the projected amounts of performance-based compensation for the firm's employees and performance-based replacement compensation for the firm's principals, as well as income taxes. A determination of a discount rate used to convert the general partner entity's compensation-adjusted after-tax cash flow into value is often challenging. As a rule of thumb, however, it is generally understood that incentive fees/carried interest are much riskier than the management fee cash flow; therefore, all else being equal, a discount rate for the incentive fees/carried interest should be higher than a discount rate for management fee cash flow. The calculations of present value of the general partner entity's cash flow should also consider the pattern of the projected cash flow, as it may influence discount conventions used in the calculations. Although the approach to valuing general partner entities of private equity funds is generally similar to that of valuing the general partner entities of hedge funds, there are several important differences. First, the private equity general partner's cash flow pattern follows the private equity fund's life cycle. Second, the timing of the private equity general partner's carried interest realizations is typically dictated by the type of the fund's portfolio proceeds allocation waterfall (i.e., "American" v. "European"). Finally, a discount rate or discount rates for the private equity general partner's cash flow may vary over the private equity fund's life cycle.

Chapter 10

Typical Challenges and Considerations in the Valuation of Hedge Funds and Private Equity Firms

Given their nature as private entities, while valuations of closely held businesses present their own set of challenges, there are certain idiosyncratic issues that particularly impact the valuation of hedge funds and private equity firms. The following sections will discuss the unique challenges and considerations with respect to most valuations of hedge funds and private equity firms. Examples of the specific challenges and considerations are as follows:

- Future investment performance and net fund flows
- Perpetual business operation assumption
- Exit dates for private equity investments
- Key person and reasonable compensation
- Legal ownership versus actual allocation of economic benefits
- Issues specific to valuations in divorce litigation, including personal goodwill

Future Investment Performance and Net Fund Flows

Value drivers for hedge fund management and general partner entities are fee-paying assets under management (AUM) and the fund's fee structure. The expected future investment performance, based on these two value drivers, is a key assumption that can have a material effect on valuation. Typical reference points for investment return expectations include, but are not limited to:

1. A fund's historical gross investment returns since inception and particularly over a historical period comparable to the projected period. While this may be a logical starting point, past performance is not a guarantee of future results. Past performance needs to be

evaluated in the context of (1) current economic events, (2) scalability of investment strategy, (3) industry growth expectations and anticipated changes, and (4) outliers present during the observed historical period.

2. Investment returns for relevant benchmarks, such as a market and/or a hedge fund strategy index over the same performance measurement period(s). However, it has been argued that it is difficult for investment managers to consistently outperform a market index. Therefore, a question the valuation expert may ask is, should the expected investment performance of a fund be based on that of a market index?
3. A risk-free rate plus an expected risk premium for the class of assets that a fund invests in. While this reference point is easy to conceptualize, it may be difficult to utilize, as risk premium data with respect to the class of assets that a fund invests in may not exist. For this investment return expectation, long-only equity and fixed income hedge fund strategies may be better suited due to the availability of data.
4. Industry, trade, or other publications that contain pricing multiples applicable to the fund's portfolio investments.
5. Pricing multiples of guideline public companies sufficiently similar to a fund's portfolio investments.

Similar to investment performance, a fund's historical net fund flows since inception and over a historical period comparable to the projected period can be a reference point when projecting future net fund flows. Further, the correlation between a fund's historical net fund flows and historical investment performance should be analyzed, as this correlation is another reference point for projected net fund flows. For instance, if it is discovered that after years of poor performance relative to the overall market or other benchmarks, the fund has net redemptions equal to 5% of AUM, this net redemption rate can be considered in developing projections of AUM. Researching both macroeconomic trends as well as the economics relative to a fund's investment portfolio can also assist a valuation expert in estimating a fund's future net fund flows. For example, during periods of strong economic growth, investor confidence may be higher, leading investors to contribute more to hedge funds and other alternative asset vehicles. On the other hand, periods of economic uncertainty and downturn may lead to poor investor confidence and investors withdrawing their investments from hedge funds. For private equity funds that were fully called and deployed as of a valuation date, net fund flows are generally not a concern, as investors' capital is locked up until the fund begins harvesting (i.e., selling) its investments.

Perpetual Business Operation Assumption

A key consideration in the valuation of hedge funds and private equity firms is the assumption of perpetual business operation. Depending on the circumstances, a perpetual life assumption may not apply, or at least needs to be explicitly evaluated in every case. In evaluating whether a hedge fund or private equity firm can operate perpetually, consider the following:

- A hedge fund's or private equity firm's performance during the observed historical period as well as projected performance. Hedge funds and private equity firms face a risk of closure in situations of persistent underperformance.
- The age and intentions of the firm's principals/owners, and their ability and willingness to transition duties to others within the firm (i.e., key person risk) in order to successfully raise new funds.
- A hedge fund's or private equity firm's longevity also depends on size of AUM, and type and diversity of investor base.

Exit Date for Private Equity Investments

The time horizon for a private equity firm to monetize a fund's underlying portfolio companies varies and could be anywhere between three and 12 years. Gaining an understanding of management's expectations as it relates to full realization (and at what multiple) of the firm's underlying portfolio assets is an essential component of the valuation analysis.

Key Person and Related Reasonable Compensation Issues

In the context of valuation, compensation of hedge fund and private equity principals presents issues that are similar to those in traditional businesses. Principals' primary compensation often comes in the form of profit distributions, rather than traditional salaries and bonuses. When principals do receive traditional compensation, it is either a base amount or it reflects the fact that these individuals are often star contributors, faces of the firms, and primary investment idea generators, without whom the business may not continue in its present form. Principals often play multiple roles in the business, including as portfolio managers, chief investment officers, chief operating officers, and chief executive officers. Therefore, normalization of reported compensation may be necessary, even when valuing a minority interest. However, due to the private nature of the industry, a practical challenge is finding reliable compensation benchmarking data.

Compensation benchmarks provided by industry-specific surveys can be a reference point for the valuation expert in determining reasonable compensation for principals of hedge funds and private equity firms.[1] For example, there are several surveys available that provide general guidelines and data on compensation in the hedge fund and private equity industries by position type, experience, fund size, and fund performance. Unsurprisingly, the data indicates that compensation depends on investment performance and the size of the fund; for example, portfolio managers' bonus compensation at high-performing funds could be as high as 50% to 60% of performance fees. Appraisers should be aware that, like other studies involving hedge funds and private equity firms, the data may have a reporting or survivorship bias.[2] When valuing hedge fund and private equity firm interests, the valuation expert should consider searching for and carefully reviewing market/industry surveys, and consider utilizing other reference points for compensation information. See Chapter 11 for a more detailed discussion of this topic.

Another potential reference point for compensation information is analyzing the compensation levels at publicly traded alternative asset management and investment banking firms. Compensation of a hedge fund's or private equity firm's principals can be thought of as having two components: (1) reasonable compensation for a given role and level of responsibility, and (2) a fair return to the principals as owners of the firm. Publicly traded firms try to balance the competing needs of various stakeholders (i.e., employees and shareholders); therefore, the observed levels of total compensation at publicly traded alternative asset management and investment banking firms may be an indication of the point of equilibrium. Reasonable compensation of principals can be estimated as the targeted total compensation, based upon publicly traded firms, less the actual compensation paid to the subject firm's non-owner employees. When considering which publicly traded firms to include in the derivation of targeted total compensation, care must be exercised in analyzing revenue due to differences in how publicly traded firms report performance fee revenue.

As hedge fund and private equity firm managers compete with other market participants for talent, compensation paid to non-owner portfolio managers at the firm may be indicative of compensation that an owner/ principal of the firm may reasonably expect to receive under hypothetical

1. It is necessary to note that, like other studies involving hedge funds and private equity firms, the data may have reporting and survivorship biases.

2. Survivorship bias is the tendency for failed companies to be excluded from performance studies because they no longer exist, thereby potentially skewing the results.

third-party ownership. However, a compensation analysis using these metrics should consider any additional or different roles and responsibilities that a principal has, compared to the non-owner portfolio managers. Compensation consultants can also provide estimates of reasonable compensation using a variety of methodologies and can utilize proprietary databases that are maintained and updated over time. Counsel should ensure that the compensation consultant is able to provide expert testimony if the matter proceeds to trial. Further, a compensation consultant can help prepare a rebuttal of the opposing expert's opinion of reasonable compensation.

Legal Ownership v. Actual Allocation of Economic Benefits

To properly value a particular interest, it is important to calculate the correct dilution based on the actual economic allocation of profits as opposed to the reported direct ownership of equity. For example, direct equity ownership might be 50%/50%, but there may be individuals that receive a 10% allocation of economic profits. Therefore, the dilution for the proper attribution of profits to all economic profit participants would be 45%/45%/10%. The economic allocation of profits should be factored into the valuation.

Family Law Business Valuation Considerations

In addition to the issues discussed earlier, there are unique considerations that may need consideration in family law matters.

Applicable Standard of Value

The standard of value (SOV) applicable in a family law matter varies by jurisdiction. The SOV may be defined by state statute or by case law. Practitioners should be aware of the applicable SOV in each jurisdiction they perform valuations in.

Valuation Date

The valuation date is also typically set by statute or case law or can be agreed upon as a stipulated cut-off date. Irrespective of the date, the principle of "known or knowable," whereby the valuation consultant can only consider anything that was known or knowable as of the valuation date, still applies. There also may be multiple valuation dates (i.e., date of marriage, date of separation, date of trial, etc.), so the valuation consultant should clearly define the scope of work at the outset of the case.

Post-Marital Efforts/Personal Goodwill

In some jurisdictions, personal goodwill—that is, an individual's personal skills, reputation, and expertise—may be their separate property and not subject to division in the divorce. In the context of a hedge fund or private equity firm, a qualitative analysis of the founders' roles, relationships, key person provisions (in the limited partnership agreement), expertise, reputation, and so on, needs to be performed in order to properly assess the potential existence of personal goodwill. Goodwill is discussed in greater detail in Chapter 12.

Applicable Case Law

The relevant case law for a given jurisdiction that defines such things as the SOV, valuation date, acceptable valuation methodologies, and determination of personal goodwill should be familiar to the valuation consultant and incorporated into their analysis as necessary and appropriate.

Summary

A valuation of an interest in a hedge fund or private equity fund requires knowledge of both the factors that are unique to the entity (such as investment exit dates, and past and expected performance) and the factors that are unique to the industry (such as compensation to principals, and legal versus economic interest allocation). While there are challenges in the valuation of hedge funds and private equity firms, a valuation consultant who considers the issues discussed in this chapter will be well prepared, whether in a family law context or other valuation scenarios.

Chapter 11

Reasonable Compensation for Key Managers/Principals[1]

Introduction

Compensation models typically determine how a firm's earnings are allocated, but they do not directly determine the amount of earnings to be allocated. However, a well-designed compensation model should enhance earnings by aligning behaviors and motivations that increase firm earnings with the compensation earned by the professionals in question. This is one reason why founders and other key employees of successful alternative asset management firms earn a disproportionate share of income.

Founder Compensation

Just like any other kind of business, the scope and scale of the management team that directs a given investment management firm varies depending upon (1) the size of the business, (2) the breadth of the firm's business lines and geographic footprint, and (3) the age of the firm. Despite the significant growth and expansion of the alternative asset management industry in the past 25 years, many firms are still managed by the founder(s), and like the founder of any business, a hedge fund/private equity firm founder's compensation often represents all or a significant portion of the firm's net profits. As firms mature and become more institutionalized and scaled, a founder's compensation typically becomes more consistent and aligned with other partners' compensation—particularly when the firm goes public or sells an equity interest in the management and general partner (GP)

1. This chapter was authored by Adam Zoia, founder and chairman of Glocap Search LLC, a talent placement firm focusing on the alternative asset management industry and a former publisher of Glocap Hedge Fund Compensation Report with Hedge Fund Research Inc.

entities to a third party, such as a GP stakes fund.[2] A founder's compensation varies materially based on the stage of the firm's development (i.e., the extent to which the founder(s) are still in charge) and across asset classes—such as hedge funds versus private equity/venture capital funds. Part of that differentiation is a reflection of the different ways in which these kinds of fund managers are compensated by their limited partners (LPs) (annual incentive fee for most hedge funds versus carried interest for private equity and venture capital funds). That is why in this chapter, senior management compensation, including founder compensation, for hedge funds versus private equity/venture capital will be discussed separately in the interest of clarity.

Hedge Funds

Hedge Fund Chief Executive Officer (Chairman, Executive Managing Member)

Given the relatively young age of the industry, there are not many hedge funds where the founder(s) is still not in charge or present in some form. As stated previously, de facto their compensation represents the firm's net profit after all other professionals are compensated and all other expenses are paid. In cases where the founders are no longer actively involved in the hedge fund, typically a chairman, chief executive officer (CEO), or executive managing member is the most senior executive at the firm and their compensation consists of:

- Base salary
- Bonus in the form of profit-sharing as a percent of the overall annual incentive fee and excess management fee.[3] Portions of this bonus may be paid out during the year, but the bulk of it is typically paid out in the first quarter of the following year once all fees have been collected and all expenses paid out (such as year-end bonuses for other team members).

CEOs of hedge funds are often intimately involved in selecting and managing the fund's portfolio positions, evaluating, guiding, and managing

2. A GP stakes fund is typically a private equity fund that specializes in investing in non-controlling interests (i.e., stakes) in management and GP entities of hedge fund and private equity management firms.

3. "Excess management fee" here indicates management fee profitability after all uses of the management fee are allocated, such as office space expenses, employee salary compensation and benefits, technology system expenses, etc.

other portfolio managers (PMs) and, if applicable, the chief investment officer (CIO). Notwithstanding the existence of a risk manager and/or department and software that often supports portfolio risk management, the CEO also is ultimately responsible for the risk profile and management of the fund's overall portfolio. The CEO also often takes the lead on evaluating and then initiating additional products or strategies for the fund and is the ultimate authority for communication with the LPs. The CEO also is the key decision-maker for discretionary compensation for senior investment staff.

Chief Investment Officer

The title and role of CIO is often found in long-only asset managers. However, as many hedge funds have become more scaled and institutionalized, the CIO role has been increasingly adopted by hedge funds. Sometimes the CIO is in line to take over from the founder when the founder retires or partially steps back and it can become a sort of CEO-under-trial scenario. Like in a long-only fund, the CIO at a hedge fund manages all of the PMs, nearly always has their own book of positions as well, and often pays close attention to the overall risk position of the fund across their various portfolios. Compensation is very similar to that of the CEO but with more weighting on the incentive fee than the excess management fee compared to the CEO compensation. For multi-asset type funds, the CIO has the added role of working with the other asset management functions within the firm on matters such as risk and fund expansion, growth and idea generation, and facilitating information sharing across asset classes and investments. The CIO is also materially involved in evaluating and selecting new PMs and other senior firm professionals such as chief legal officer, chief risk officer, chief operating officer, chief financial officer, chief marketing officer, chief human resources officer, and the like.

Portfolio Manager

Most funds have a number of PMs, depending upon the fund's scale and overall strategy. A PM is the senior-most fund management position after CEO and CIO. There are multi-manager hedge funds where multiple PMs manage a slice of the overall fund portfolio, often with their own dedicated team of analysts ("multi-manager funds"), and there are single portfolio hedge funds where the CEO, CIO, or their equivalent has the final say on PM investment decisions ("single portfolio funds"). In both kinds of funds, PMs often have an investment team working with them, usually on a dedicated basis, consisting of analysts and research associates—all of whom participate in specific ways toward selecting and then managing positions in the portfolio. The primary job of a PM is to select, size, and manage positions, including, where applicable, applying hedging and other risk management techniques.

Multi-Manager PMs

In most multi-manager funds, individual PMs typically focus on different investment areas.[4] PMs in these funds typically earn a base salary and a bonus, which usually represents a fixed percentage of the investment firm's incentive fee and, in some cases, the management fee, earned on the specific portion of the fund's portfolio managed by a PM.[5]

For most funds, a GP's incentive fees are subject to a high-water mark, which means that over a specified period, if incentive fees are paid out to the GP and then subsequently a fund loses money, the fund has to recoup those losses before the GP can earn incentive fees again. In the presence of high-water mark provisions, some portion of the PM's payouts in strong years is often held back and deferred to take into account the potential for a down year in subsequent years where technically the PM would have negative earnings pursuant to their internal PM contracts. These holdbacks to PM payouts help the fund in equalizing for any such LP fee deductions over a multi-year period.

In multi-manager funds, each PM's capital allocation over which the PM can exercise investment discretion is often capped. Capital allocations, which can adjust periodically based on a fund's assets under management (AUM) and investment performance, are one of the tools investment firms use to recruit PMs that can materially affect a PM's compensation potential. In addition, PMs' payouts are often reduced by the direct costs of the PM's dedicated investment team (senior analysts, analysts, research associates) and allocation of firmwide overhead, such as data costs, research expenses, and other specific business expenses.

Single-Manager PMs

In funds that operate as a single investment portfolio, the job of the PM is to originate and advocate for potentially profitable portfolio investments. In these funds, PMs often specialize in a certain industry vertical (e.g.,

---

4. These investment areas, representing slices of a fund's overall portfolio, may be organized by industry (i.e., healthcare, technology, financial services, etc.), asset type (i.e., equities, credit, crypto, etc.), investment strategy, or some other characteristic.

5. The individual PM's compensation may be subject to limitations or reallocation based on the fund's overall performance and netting risk considerations for winning and losing investment teams.

healthcare) or asset type (e.g., credit). Although in these firms the CIO or CEO usually has the ultimate authority over the investment decisions, PMs often still have a certain degree of flexibility to make allocation decisions without formal approval from the CIO or CEO within the PM's vertical/asset type. For single-manager PMs, compensation typically consists of a base salary and discretionary bonus. Depending upon the degree of PM autonomy, the bonus may be (1) calculated, in part or in whole, as a percentage of the firm's incentive fee, or (2) determined on a discretionary basis by the CIO or CEO based on the assessment of the PM's relative contribution to the fund's performance. In either case, the bonus structure typically considers the PM's contribution over time, longevity, and the fund and competitive dynamics for the PM position in the marketplace.

Figure 11.1 summarizes typical compensation structures for select hedge fund executive roles.

Figure 11.1
Hedge Funds

Senior, Key Position	Summary of Role	Core Compensation Structure
Chairman/CEO/ Executive Managing Member	Often firm founder; final decision-maker in fund but typically does not weigh in on or make every investment decision; spearheads firm expansion plans both in terms of AUM and fund strategies	1. Base salary 2. Percentage of the firm's overall profits (incentive fee + management fee)
CIO	In charge of PMs and overall portfolio; this position does not exist in all hedge funds	1. Base salary 2. Percentage of the firm's overall incentive fee and excess management fee earnings
PM	Manages a portion of the fund's AUM typically with a team of senior analysts and analysts; typically within firm confines is responsible for choosing, sizing, and exiting and/or hedging positions in their portfolio	1. Base salary 2. Discretionary bonus or for multi-manager firms, a percentage of the incentive fee earned by the firm on PM's separate portfolio

Private Equity and Venture Capital Funds

Managing Partner/Senior Partner

Many private equity and venture capital funds were founded by two (or more) investment professionals and in such cases, there might be two managing partners as opposed to one. The job of the managing partner is not unlike that of a CEO of any business—to manage the overall business. The managing partner always sits on the investment committee, helps recruit and screen senior and other firm professionals, and is often the critical individual managing LP relationships in conjunction with dedicated team members within the firm. The managing partner also takes the lead on considering new business lines for the firm such as new asset classes and also manages the other GPs in the business.

Compensation typically consists of a base salary and a percentage of the firm's net profits or otherwise a set percentage of the carried interest and excess management fee (i.e., of the firm's overall profitability).

General Partner/Partner

At a private equity/venture capital firm, the partners (technically, GPs or members/partners of a GP entity) are focused, in part, on (1) originating, evaluating, and negotiating new potential investments; (2) participating in the investment committee where the fund's partners evaluate new potential investment opportunities; (3) securing financing (and/or bringing in other equity investors if the deal size so requires) for new deals and for add-on acquisitions; (4) managing, guiding, and directing junior investment professionals; and (5) sitting on portfolio company boards and otherwise working closely with portfolio companies. Depending upon the nature of the investment (i.e., venture, growth equity, or later-stage private equity), partners may get involved in the private equity firm's strategy, often working with the CEO. Partners also help find and evaluate potential new hires for the firm.

Partner compensation consists of a base salary plus a share of the carried interest in the fund. In some cases, partners may also share in a portion of the excess management fee (i.e., the management entity's net profits). In some cases, there can be discretionary cash bonuses for partners, which are often decided by the managing partner based on such performance criteria as deal origination, deal exits where the partner in question played a material part (i.e., was a lead partner for the portfolio company), or other performance metrics, such as training and development of junior staff.

Figure 11.2 summarizes typical compensation structures for select executive roles at private equity and venture capital firms.

Figure 11.2

Private Equity and Venture Capital Funds

Key Position	Role	Compensation
Managing Partner/ Senior Partner	Often firm founder, manages the overall business including fundraising, chairs the investment committee, manages the other GPs, takes the lead on business expansion	Base salary + annual profit-sharing in the overall firm's performance from carried interest and management fees (i.e., a portion of firm profit after all other expenses are paid) + no-fee co-investment opportunities in firm deals
GP	Helps to originate new deals, takes the lead in evaluating new deals and add-on investments, manages the more junior investment professionals, sits on boards of portfolio companies, participates and votes in investment committee that discusses potential new deals	Base salary, discretionary bonus + portion of carried interest + opportunity to invest in the fund and/or specific deals on a preferred basis (often without normal charges of carried interest or management fees that LPs pay)

Publicly Traded Funds

As the alternative asset management industry continues to mature, it is increasingly common for investment firms to go public. Firms that have become public include private equity-focused firms such as Apollo, KKR, Blackstone, Ares, and Hamilton Lane, as well as hedge fund managers, such as Sculptor and Man Group. In a typical initial public offering (IPO), the legal structure of the business often changes, and stock options and stock ownership can become additional components of compensation for certain investment professionals within the now publicly traded fund management company. For privately held firms, compensation components are typically base salary (along with usual benefits) and variable compensation, such as carried interest, which for senior personnel is mostly tied to performance of their portfolio and/or the firm overall. For publicly traded firms, there is a third compensation component—public equity awards. For most investment management firms, publicly traded equity is held by founders and other senior executives, and as these individuals retire or leave the business, equity is often transferred to professionals who assume those roles through some form of buyout over time of the departing owners from the business. At publicly traded firms, employees often receive stock option grants that are subject to vesting requirements just like at any other publicly traded company. Sometimes the grants of equity-linked entitlements include stock appreciation rights (SARs), nonqualified stock options (NSOs), and incentive stock options (ISOs). The vesting schedules often have a time-based component (say, four to five years) and a performance-based component.

Summary

An effective compensation model for key managers in private equity and hedge funds motivates behavior that increases a firm's overall profitability, rather than merely dividing existing profits. Founders typically receive a large share of the profits early in a firm's life cycle, as they are deeply involved in managing investments, strategy, and investor relationships. However, as firms mature, institutionalize, or sell interests to third parties, founder compensation usually aligns closer to other partners, with variations depending on asset classes: hedge fund compensation emphasizes annual incentive fees, while private equity and venture capital compensation centers on carried interest.

Hedge fund CEOs—often the original founders—generally receive a salary combined with a defined portion of annual incentive and excess management fees, with responsibilities spanning portfolio risk management, investor relations, product expansion, and senior-level bonuses. CIOs, typically present in larger, institutionalized hedge funds, have similar pay structures but with a greater emphasis on incentive fees. PMs' compensation varies: multi-manager PMs earn a salary plus a fixed percentage of incentive fees on their own portfolio performance, often net of team costs and subject to holdbacks related to high-water mark provisions, while single-manager PMs receive a base salary and discretionary bonuses determined by firm leadership based on their contributions and market conditions.

Private equity and venture capital funds feature managing partners who function as CEOs, managing operations, investment decisions, and investor relations. They typically receive a salary plus a significant share of profits or incentive fees. GPs are compensated with a base salary and carried interest, sometimes supplemented by excess management fees or performance-based bonuses. For publicly traded alternative asset firms, compensation further includes equity components—such as stock options or direct share ownership—vesting over time or based on performance, and sometimes equity in portfolio companies, providing long-term alignment between key personnel and firm success.

Chapter 12

Personal v. Enterprise Goodwill

Introduction

In this chapter, you will learn about:

- Differences in characteristics between personal (professional) and enterprise (entity) goodwill
- How personal goodwill can impact a divorce case involving a hedge fund or private equity firm
- Relevant case law decisions on the issue of personal goodwill

The distinction between personal and enterprise goodwill is becoming an increasingly important aspect of business valuation. This is primarily true in conjunction with marital dissolution matters, as an increasing number of states are requiring a separation of personal goodwill from enterprise goodwill, with many excluding personal goodwill from the marital estate. This distinction can also be a significant factor in corporate taxation, where the source of proceeds from a sale can be considered personal goodwill and therefore not typically subject to taxation.

At last count prior to publication, the latest court cases in 30 states and the District of Columbia now include enterprise goodwill as part of the marital estate in a dissolution but exclude personal goodwill. Louisiana has even passed a statute to that effect.

The number of states whose recent court case rulings included both enterprise and personal goodwill as part of the marital estate has shrunk to 13. The remaining states have more complex components in determining whether goodwill should be included in the marital estate, including factors such as marketability or salability, whether the business is a professional practice, or whether the professional will continue to practice.[1]

1. Business Valuation Resources, *Charting Goodwill Jurisprudence + Map* (April 2019).

Personal Goodwill

In some jurisdictions, personal goodwill and an individual's personal skills, reputation, and expertise may be their separate property and not subject to division in a divorce. As discussed in Chapter 11, in the context of a hedge fund or private equity firm, a qualitative analysis of the founders' roles, relationships, key person provisions (in the limited partnership agreement), expertise, reputation, and so on needs to be performed in order to properly assess the potential existence of personal goodwill.

The existence of a noncompete agreement may be an indicium of personal goodwill in the context of marital dissolution. Similarly, covenants not to compete are categorized by most, but not all, states as a personal asset not subject to distribution, due to their restrictions on the future activities of the spouse.[2] Arguably, a covenant not to compete can be a mechanism for buyers to contractually effectuate the transfer of an individual's personal goodwill.

Distinction Between Enterprise and Personal Goodwill

Goodwill is an intangible asset that contributes to earnings as a result of a host of intangible assets including name, reputation, customer and employee loyalty, location, products, and similar factors not separately identified. It is the expectancy of repeat patronage. The issue in distinguishing enterprise from personal goodwill is what or who is generating that expectancy of repeat patronage.

Enterprise (business or entity) goodwill is the part of goodwill that is attributable to the entity as opposed to the individual. Goodwill is the total value of an enterprise, less its tangible and identifiable intangible value. Enterprise goodwill is an intangible asset owned by and associated with the operation of the business entity and can include the business's locations, customer base, trained workforce, reputation, product brands, and name.

Personal goodwill is the part of goodwill that is attributable to the individual as opposed to the entity. Personal goodwill is owned by a shareholder or employee and exists when that person's skills, reputation, expertise, knowledge, and relationships with customers, suppliers, vendors, employees, and so on directly contribute to the company's success.

---

2. *Kricsfeld v. Kricsfeld*, 588 N.W.2d 210 (Neb. Ct. App. 1999). Nebraska's court of appeals looked to other jurisdictions and concluded that the covenant not to compete is not a marital asset.

Personal goodwill is associated with specialized skills, personal relationships, and reputation of the owners as opposed to the name and reputation of the organization itself. Simply stated, for enterprise goodwill to exist, it must be institutionalized with recognition of the business and not be primarily attributable to any individual(s). In practice, it is not unusual for a business to have elements of both enterprise and personal goodwill. In those instances, an allocation is usually made between both elements. Other identifiable intangible assets like trademarks, patents, assembled workforce, and favorable contracts should also be considered.

An analysis of whether the goodwill of a business is enterprise or personal or some combination of both begins with a thorough understanding of the business. This includes reviewing detailed job descriptions for management, and an analysis of customer relationships and the level of competition.

Enterprise Goodwill Characteristics

The following characteristics are generally indicative of enterprise goodwill:

- Company has written contracts with major customers.
- Company has written contracts with major suppliers.
- Company has written employment and/or noncompete agreements with key employees.
- It is a large business with formalized organizational structure, systems, and controls.
- Company has formalized production methods and business systems.
- Business or practice is not heavily dependent on personal service performed by the owner(s).
- Company sales result from company name recognition and/or salesforce as opposed to name and reputation of key individuals.
- Company has an advantageous location(s).
- Company itself has brand recognition.
- It is viewed by both customers and suppliers as an enterprise.

Personal Goodwill Characteristics

As implied by the word "personal," this intangible asset is the capitalized income stream or cost savings generated solely by a key employee who lacks an employment contract and/or noncompete agreement. Personal goodwill exists if the loss of that key person would reduce the future revenue and/or profits of the business for some period. This is referred to as a valuation "with and without" the key person.

The following characteristics are generally indicative of personal goodwill:

- It is an entrepreneurial business highly dependent on owner's personal skills, knowledge, reputation, personality, expertise, and relationships.
- There are no noncompete or employment agreements.
- Personal services provided by the owner(s) are an important feature in the company's products or services.
- Personal know-how exists.
- Sales and performance are largely dependent on owner's personal relationship with customers and reputation.
- Product and/or services know-how and supplier relationships rest primarily with the owner(s).

Case Examples

Divorce Cases[3]

By way of example, the following are two cases in which personal goodwill was at issue. In a large neuropsychiatry practice, the doctor, who owned 100% of the stock, had largely institutionalized the goodwill (i.e., enterprise goodwill). The company had a staff of about 60 doctors and therapists, some as employees and some as independent contractors. It had employment and noncompete agreements with all the department heads and key doctors. It also had contracts with all the hospitals it serviced, and most of the doctors had their own patient relationships. The doctor/owner personally saw few patients, but he negotiated contracts with hospitals and hired all the key professionals. The court concluded that the goodwill was 70% institutional (i.e., enterprise) and 30% personal.

A specialized niche insurance agency was the opposite. The president had personal relationships with all the underwriters and most of the larger customers. He had also developed very loyal relationships with all the largest producing agents. The agency had no contracts with any customers and no employment or noncompete agreements. In this case, most of the goodwill was found to be personal.

3. Shannon P. Pratt and Alina V. Niculita, "The Distinction Between Personal and Enterprise Goodwill," *Family Lawyer Magazine* (June 17, 2022).

Income Tax Cases

In the landmark *Martin Ice Cream* decision,[4] an individual named Strassberg was the first distributor of Häagen-Dazs ice cream. He had successfully placed Häagen-Dazs ice cream in a significant number of large grocery chains. When Pillsbury acquired Häagen-Dazs, the acquisition included all distributor rights. The Internal Revenue Service (IRS) determined there was a large enterprise-level intangible asset related to the distributor rights. However, the court ruled that most of the value of the distributorship was personal to Strassberg, the stockholder, which saved a large amount of tax at the corporate level.

In *Norwalk*,[5] another landmark decision, an accounting firm liquidated, and an IRS agent determined there had been a liquidating distribution of enterprise-level intangible assets, so the IRS agent assessed a tax on approximately $600,000 of corporate gain on the distribution. However, because there was no noncompete agreement between the shareholders and the accounting firm, the court ruled that all the otherwise enterprise-level intangibles that the IRS had deemed distributed at the time of the liquidation were, in fact, personal goodwill. The court stated:

> We find no authority which holds that an individual's ability is part of the assets of a corporation by which he is employed where, as in the instant case, the corporation does not have a right by contract or otherwise to the future services of the individuals.[6]

These are only two examples of many cases that include the issue of personal goodwill. Lawyers and valuation professionals should be familiar with the qualitative factors included in case law applicable to the jurisdiction in which the matter is filed.

Summary

The classification of an intangible asset as personal goodwill could have a material impact on the financial outcome of a divorce or the taxation of the sale of a business. First, knowledge of the applicable statutes and case law is necessary to determine whether personal goodwill is a marital asset or not, or taxable as a separate asset. Next, if personal goodwill is to be carved

4. *Martin Ice Cream Co. v. Commissioner*, 110 T.C. 189 (1998).
5. *Norwalk v. Commissioner*, T.C. Memo. 1998-279 (1998).
6. *Ibid.*

out of the marital estate or purchase price allocation, the valuation expert needs to perform a credible analysis in order to present persuasive testimony and valuable evidence to the court or IRS.

References for Personal v. Enterprise Goodwill

Business Valuation Resources, *Business Valuation in Divorce Case Law Compendium*, 5th ed. (Portland, OR: Business Valuation Resources, 2020).

———. *BVR's Guide to Personal v. Enterprise Goodwill*, 5th ed. (Portland, OR: Business Valuation Resources, 2012).

———. *Valuing Goodwill in Divorce* (Portland, OR: Business Valuation Resources, 2011).

Hitchner, James R, "Trifurcation of Goodwill and the Concept of Tradeable Personal Goodwill," and "Personal Goodwill in Commercial Businesses," in *Financial Valuation: Applications and Models*, 4th ed., edited by James R. Hitchner (Hoboken, NJ: John Wiley & Sons, 2017).

Laro, David, and Shannon P. Pratt, "Personal Versus Enterprise Goodwill," in *Business Valuation and Federal Taxes: Procedure, Law, and Perspective*, 2nd ed. (Hoboken, NJ: John Wiley & Sons, 2011), 333–42.

Pratt, Shannon P., and ASA Educational Foundation, "Goodwill and Going-Concern Value" and "Goodwill," in *Shannon Pratt's Valuing a Business: The Analysis and Appraisal of Closely Held Businesses*, 6th ed. (New York, NY: McGraw-Hill, 2022), 572–76 and 1036–46.

Trugman, Gary R., "Professional Versus Practice Goodwill," in *Understanding Business Valuations*, 6th ed. (Portland, OR: Business Valuation Resources, 2022), 817–43.

Wood, David, "'MUM's the Word': A Formal Method to Allocate Blue Sky Value in Divorce," *Business Valuation Update* (March 2007).

Chapter 13

Accounting and Tax Issues Related to Hedge Funds and Private Equity Firms[1]

Understanding Partnership Taxation

The foundation for understanding the taxation of hedge funds, private equity, and venture capital firms (referred to herein as alternative asset managers, or AAMs) lies in grasping the concept of partnership taxation. Unlike corporations, which are separate taxpaying entities, partnerships are generally not taxed at the entity level. Instead, they are considered "pass-through" entities.

Pass-Through Taxation

In a pass-through taxation system, the partnership itself does not pay taxes on its income. Instead, all the partnership's income, deductions, credits, and losses pass through to the individual partners. Each partner then reports their share of these items on their personal tax returns.

As an illustration, let's consider a hedge fund management firm structured as a partnership that earns $100 million in a year and has 100 equal partners:

- The hedge fund firm itself will not pay any tax on this $100 million.
- Each partner would report $1 million of income on their individual tax returns.
- This is true regardless of whether the partnership actually distributed this money to the partners or not.

This pass-through structure has several important implications:

1. **Single layer of taxation**. Unlike corporations, where profits are taxed at the corporate level and then again when distributed to

1. This chapter was authored by Leo Berg, CPA, senior manager, and Lyle Kotler, CPA, managing director of the Alternative Investment Group of CBIZ Financial Services.

shareholders as dividends (known as "double taxation"), partnership profits are only taxed once, at the individual partner level. This can result in significant tax savings to the partnership.

2. **Character preservation**. The character of income (whether capital gains, ordinary income, or tax-exempt income) is generally preserved as it passes through to the partners. For instance, if the partnership realizes long-term capital gains, the partners report long-term capital gains on their individual returns, potentially benefiting from preferential (i.e., lower) tax rates.
3. **Timing of taxation**. Partners must report their share of partnership income in the year income is earned by the partnership, even if income is not distributed to them. This can sometimes result in "phantom income"—taxable income without corresponding cash distributions. This can be particularly relevant for an AAM, where profits might be reinvested rather than distributed.
4. **Flexibility in allocations**. Partnerships have significant flexibility in how they allocate income, gains, losses, and deductions among partners, as long as the allocations have "substantial economic effect."[2]
5. **Complexity**. While pass-through taxation can offer benefits, it also introduces complexity. Partners must track their basis in the partnership, deal with complex allocation rules, and potentially file tax returns in multiple states or countries where the partnership operates.

To illustrate the concepts, let's consider a simple example: Suppose a private equity fund structured as a partnership has two partners: a general partner (the private equity firm) and a limited partner (an investor). In a given year, the fund realizes the following:

- $5 million in long-term capital gains from selling a portfolio company
- $1 million in ordinary income from interest and dividends
- $500,000 in short-term capital gains from a short-term investment
- $200,000 in deductible expenses

Continuing with our illustration, let's also assume that the partnership agreement allocates 20% of profits to the general partner (as carried

2. The Internal Revenue Service does not simply accept any allocation scheme the partners devise. Under section 704(b) of the Internal Revenue Code (IRC), allocations in the partnership agreement are respected for tax purposes only if they have "substantial economic effect."

interest) and 80% to the limited partner. The tax implications would be as follows:

General partner:

- $1 million in long-term capital gains (20% of $5 million)
- $200,000 in ordinary income (20% of $1 million)
- $100,000 in short-term capital gains (20% of $500,000)
- $40,000 in deductions (20% of $200,000)

Limited partner:

- $4 million in long-term capital gains (80% of $5 million)
- $800,000 in ordinary income (80% of $1 million)
- $400,000 in short-term capital gains (80% of $500,000)
- $160,000 in deductions (80% of $200,000)

Each partner would report these amounts on their individual tax returns, preserving the character of each type of income and deduction.

Contrast Pass-Through Entities with C Corporations

As stated earlier in this chapter, pass-through entities, in the context of taxation, are business structures that do not pay corporate income tax. Instead, the profits and losses of the business "pass through" to the owners or partners, who report their share of the business's income on their personal tax returns. The most common types of pass-through entities are general partnerships, limited partnerships (LPs), or limited liability partnerships (LLPs). It is worth noting that some entities, like limited liability companies (LLCs), can choose to be taxed as partnerships.

Partnerships offer significant flexibility in terms of management structure and profit allocation, making them attractive for complex business arrangements like an AAM. For an AAM, the choice of entity involves not just tax considerations but also regulatory compliance (e.g., with Securities and Exchange Commission regulations).

Unlike pass-through entities, traditional C corporations face "double taxation":

- The corporation pays corporate income tax on its profits.
- Shareholders pay personal income tax on dividends received from the corporation.

In contrast, pass-through taxation offers several advantages:

- There is a single layer of taxation: income is only taxed once, at the individual level.

- There is potential for a lower overall tax burden: depending on individual tax rates and other factors, pass-through taxation can result in an overall lower total tax liability.

Pass-through taxation has significant implications for partners:

- **Tax planning**. Partners need to plan for tax payments, as they may need to make estimated tax payments throughout the year even if they do not receive distributions of their share of income.
- **Personal tax impact**. A partner's share of business income can significantly affect their personal tax situation, potentially pushing them into higher tax brackets.
- **Basis tracking**. Partners must carefully track their basis in the partnership, which affects the tax treatment of distributions and the ability to deduct losses.

Formation and Operation of the Fund

Partnership Agreement and Allocations

The partnership agreement is a crucial document that outlines the rights and responsibilities of partners and sets the rules for the partnership's operation. In the context of an AAM, key elements often include:

- **Partnership structure**: Defining the type of partnership (e.g., general partnership, LP) and the roles of different partners (general partners, limited partners)
- **Management and control**: Outlining decision-making processes, voting rights, and the powers of general partners or managing members
- **Profit and loss allocation**: Specifying how profits, losses, and other tax items will be allocated among partners
- **Distribution waterfall**: Detailing the order and method by which cash or assets will be distributed to partners
- **Capital accounts**: Explaining how capital accounts will be maintained and adjusted
- **Admission and withdrawal of partners**: Procedures for admitting new partners and handling partner exits
- **Transfer restrictions**: Rules governing the transfer of partnership interests
- **Dissolution and liquidation**: Circumstances under which the partnership may be dissolved and the process for winding up its affairs

- **Dispute resolution**: Methods for resolving conflicts between partners
- **Confidentiality and noncompete clauses**: Particularly important for hedge funds and private equity firms to protect proprietary strategies and prevent partners from competing with the firm
- **Capital contributions by partners**
- **Types of contributions**: Partners may contribute cash, property, or services (though service contributions often have special tax implications)
- **Timing of contributions**: Initial contributions and provisions for additional capital calls
- **Valuation of non-cash contributions**: Methods for valuing property or other non-cash assets contributed to the partnership
- **Impact on capital accounts**: How contributions affect a partner's capital account and ownership percentage
- **Treatment of contribution-related liabilities**: Handling of liabilities associated with contributed property
- **Special allocations related to contributed property**: Provisions for allocating built-in gain or loss on contributed property
- **Economic v. tax allocations**: Distinguishing between allocations for economic purposes and those for tax purposes
- **Basic allocation methods**: Pro rata based on capital contributions, or more complex formulas
- **Special allocations**: Provisions for allocating certain items differently from the general allocation method
- **Substantial economic effect**: Ensuring allocations comply with Internal Revenue Service (IRS) regulations to be respected for tax purposes
- **Catch-up allocations**: Common in private equity for returning initial capital contributions before profit sharing begins
- **Carried interest allocations**: Specific provisions for allocating profits to fund managers as performance-based compensation
- **Loss limitation provisions**: Addressing limitations on loss allocations due to insufficient basis, at-risk amounts, or passive activity rules
- **Regulatory considerations**: Ensuring allocation provisions comply with relevant securities laws and regulations
- **Reallocation mechanisms**: Provisions for adjusting allocations retroactively, such as clawback provisions in private equity
- **Tax distributions**: Provisions for mandatory distributions to cover partners' tax liabilities on allocated income

Special Profit Allocations

Partnerships have flexibility to make "special allocations" that differ from the partners' overall ownership percentages. For example, a private equity firm might allocate a higher percentage of gains from a particular investment to the general partner as a form of incentive compensation (i.e., carried interest). These special allocations must still satisfy the substantial economic effect test. They are common in private equity funds, where different investments might have different economic arrangements.

For instance, a private equity fund might have a provision that allocates a higher percentage of profits to the general partner for investments that achieve a certain internal rate of return (IRR) as carried interest. This incentivizes the general partner to pursue higher performing investments.

Carried Interest

"Carried interest" is a particularly important concept for AAMs. It represents a special profits allocation based on performance where the fund managers (general partner) receive a share of the fund's profits (typically 20%) as compensation for their services.

Historically, carried interest has often been taxed at preferential, lower long-term capital gains rates, rather than as ordinary income. This has been a subject of controversy and legislative attention. Critics argue that carried interest is more akin to compensation for services (which is typically taxed at higher tax rates as ordinary income) rather than a return on invested capital.

Recent changes (section 1061 of the Internal Revenue Code (the Code)) have extended the holding period required for long-term capital gain treatment of carried interest from one year to three years for many investment partnerships. This means that to qualify for the lower long-term capital gains tax rate, the underlying investment must be held for more than three years. Let's consider an example:

A private equity fund acquires a company for $100 million. The fund agreement includes a 20% carried interest provision for the general partner (the private equity firm). After four years, the company is sold for $200 million, resulting in a $100 million gain. The allocation (assuming all priority LP distributions have been made) would be:

- Limited partners (80%): $80 million
- General partner (20% carried interest): $20 million

Prior to the changes under section 1061, the entire $20 million would have been taxed as long-term capital gain. Now, because the investment was held for more than three years, it still qualifies for long-term capital gain treatment.

However, if the investment had been sold after only two years, the $20 million would be taxed as short-term capital gain (i.e., at higher ordinary income rates) under the new rules. These rules add complexity to tax planning for private equity firms and can impact investment holding periods and exit strategies.

Contributions

When a hedge fund or private equity firm is formed, the initial partners contribute capital to get the venture started. This contribution can be in the form of cash, property, or services. The tax treatment of these initial contributions is governed by section 721 of the Code. In general, when property or cash is contributed to a partnership, no gain or loss is recognized by either the partner or the partnership.

Cash Contributions

When a partner contributes cash to the partnership, it is straightforward from a tax perspective. The partner's initial basis in their partnership interest is equal to the amount of cash contributed, and no gain or loss is recognized.

For example, if an investor contributes $10 million in cash to a newly formed hedge fund, their initial basis in their partnership interest would be $10 million. This basis becomes important for future tax calculations, including the treatment of distributions and the ability to deduct losses.

Property Contributions

If a partner contributes property (such as securities or real estate) to the partnership, the transaction is generally tax-free under section 721. The partner's initial basis in their partnership interest is equal to their basis in the contributed property, and the partnership's basis in the property (known as "inside basis") is the same as the contributing partner's basis. This rule can lead to some interesting tax planning opportunities and challenges. Consider this example: An investor wants to contribute to a private equity fund. They own shares in a publicly traded company that they purchased years ago for $1 million, shares which are now worth $5 million. They have two options:

Option 1: Sell the shares and contribute cash.

- They would recognize a $4 million capital gain on the sale.
- They would contribute $5 million cash to the partnership, giving them a $5 million basis in their partnership interest.

Option 2: Contribute the shares directly to the partnership.

- No gain is recognized on the contribution.
- Their basis in their partnership interest would be $1 million.
- The partnership's basis in the shares would be $1 million.
- The $4 million of built-in gain is preserved and will be recognized when the partnership eventually sells the shares.

Option 2 allows for deferral of the $4 million gain, which can be valuable. However, it also means that the investor's basis in their partnership interest is lower, which could impact future distributions and loss deductions.[3]

Service Contributions

Partners who contribute only services (common for the founders/managers of hedge funds and private equity firms) generally start with a zero basis in their partnership interest. However, if they receive a capital interest in exchange for services, they recognize taxable income equal to the value of the interest received, which then becomes their basis.

This is particularly relevant for AAM managers who often receive both a management fee (for services) and a carried interest (a share of profits).

Tax Basis—Tracking

Tax basis is an important concept in accounting and finance that refers to the original value of an asset for tax purposes. This value is used to determine gain or loss when the asset is sold.

Points one and two that follow provide a simplified way of explaining the concept. Points three and four explain the implication for calculating taxable gain or loss and for tax reporting.

1. **Initial value**. The tax basis generally starts with the initial purchase price of the asset. For example, if you buy a piece of equipment for $1,000, your tax basis on that equipment is $1,000.

3. There are special rules (under section 704(c)) to ensure that the built-in gain or loss at the time of contribution is ultimately allocated to a contributing partner.

2. **Adjustments**. Over time, the tax basis can be adjusted for various reasons. Common adjustments include:
   a. **Improvements**. If you spend money to improve the asset, that amount is added to the basis.
   b. **Depreciation**. If the asset loses value over time due to wear and tear (like machinery), the amount of depreciation is subtracted from the basis.
3. **Realized gain or loss**. When you sell the asset, you compare the sale price to the adjusted tax basis to calculate your realized gain or loss.
   a. **Gain**. If the sale price is higher than the adjusted tax basis, the difference is a gain.
   b. **Loss**. If the sale price is lower than the adjusted tax basis, the difference is a loss.
4. **Tax implications**. The IRS (or other taxing authority) uses your gain or loss to determine how much tax you owe or if you can take a deduction. Gains may be subject to capital gains tax, while losses may be used to offset other income.

For example:

- You bought equipment for $1,000.
- You later spent $200 on improvements, making the basis $1,200.
- You sold the equipment for $1,500.
- Your gain is $1,500 – $1,200 = $300.

Understanding tax basis is essential for accurately reporting transactions and fulfilling tax obligations.

Basis tracking is also crucial because it determines:

1. **The number of losses a partner can deduct**. A partner can only deduct losses up to their basis in the partnership in any given year. Any excess losses are suspended and carried forward to future years.
2. **The tax treatment of partnership distributions**. Cash distributions in excess of the basis are generally taxable as capital gain.
3. **The gain or loss recognized when a partner sells their interest**. When a partner sells their partnership interest, their basis is used to determine the taxable gain or loss on the sale.

How to Determine Basis

As mentioned earlier, a partner's initial basis is generally:

- **For cash contributions**: The amount of cash contributed

- **For property contributions**: The partner's basis in the contributed property
- **For service contributions**: Usually zero, unless a capital interest is received[4]

A partner's basis is then adjusted over time:
Increases to basis:

- Partner's distributive share of taxable and tax-exempt income
- Partner's increased share of partnership liabilities
- Additional contributions to the partnership

Decreases to basis:

- Distributions to the partner
- Partner's distributive share of partnership losses
- Partner's decreased share of partnership liabilities
- Nondeductible expenditures of the partnership that are not capital expenditures

Let's walk through an example to illustrate these concepts: Suppose an investor contributes $1 million to a hedge fund at the beginning of the year. Throughout the year, the following occurs:

1. The fund allocates $200,000 of taxable income to the investor.
2. The fund makes a $50,000 cash distribution to the investor.
3. The fund takes out a loan, increasing the investor's share of partnership liabilities by $100,000.
4. The fund allocates $30,000 of nondeductible expenses to the investor.

The investor's basis at the end of the year would be calculated as follows:
Initial basis: $1,000,000

+ Taxable income allocation: $200,000
- Cash distribution: ($50,000)
+ Increase in share of liabilities: $100,000
- Nondeductible expenses: ($30,000)
Ending basis: $1,220,000

For hedge funds with frequent redemptions and private equity firms with long-term investments and complex waterfall structures, accurate basis tracking is both essential and challenging.

---

4. Profits interest grants are generally tax-free.

The following three scenarios are illustrative.

Scenario 1: Loss limitation. A hedge fund partner has a basis of $500,000 in their partnership interest. In a bad year, the fund allocates a $700,000 loss to the partner. The partner can only deduct $500,000 of this loss (their basis amount). The remaining $200,000 is suspended and carried forward to future years when the partner has sufficient basis to absorb it.

** Limiting losses to the partner's adjusted basis is designed to prevent partners from deducting more losses than their financial investment in the partnership. This rule aligns with the tax principle that a taxpayer should not receive tax benefits greater than their actual economic investment.*

Scenario 2: Taxable distribution. A private equity fund partner has a basis of $1 million. The fund makes a distribution of $1.2 million to the partner. The first $1 million is a tax-free return of basis, but the extra $200,000 is treated as capital gain and is subject to tax.

Scenario 3: Sale of partnership interest. A hedge fund partner with a basis of $800,000 sells their interest for $1.5 million. They would recognize a gain of $700,000 ($1.5 million - $800,000) on the sale.

These scenarios underscore the importance of accurate basis tracking. For funds with hundreds or thousands of partners and complex allocations, this can be a significant administrative challenge.

Additional Loss Limitations

At-Risk Rules

In addition to the basis limitation illustrated in Scenario 1, the at-risk rules found in section 465 of the Code may further limit a partner's ability to deduct losses from the partnership. The at-risk rules are designed to prevent taxpayers from deducting losses in excess of their economic investment in an activity.

Under these rules, a partner is generally considered at risk for:

- Money and adjusted basis of property contributed to the activity
- Amounts borrowed for use in the activity for which the partner is personally liable
- The partner's share of qualified nonrecourse financing

A partner can only deduct losses from an activity to the extent of their amount at risk in the activity at the end of the tax year. Losses in excess of the at-risk amount are suspended and carried forward to future years. These rules can be particularly relevant for hedge funds using leverage and for private equity firms using debt financing in their portfolio companies. For example, At-Risk Limitation Partner J invests $100,000 in a hedge fund. The fund borrows an additional $900,000 on a nonrecourse basis (i.e., Partner J is not personally liable for the debt). In the first year, the fund allocates a $150,000 loss to Partner J.
Result:

- Partner J's amount at risk is $100,000 (their cash contribution).
- Partner J can deduct $100,000 of the loss.
- The remaining $50,000 loss is suspended and carried forward.

Passive Activity Rules

In addition to the basis and at-risk limitations, partners must also contend with the passive activity loss rules under section 469 of the Code. These rules generally limit a taxpayer's ability to deduct losses from passive activities against nonpassive income. These rules were enacted in order to curtail the use of tax shelters, where taxpayers could invest in activities that generated large tax losses to offset other forms of income, thus significantly reducing their overall tax liability. For most limited partners in hedge funds and private equity firms, their investment will be considered a passive activity. This means that losses can generally only offset passive income from other sources.

However, these rules are complex and have many exceptions. For instance, certain types of working interests in oil and gas properties are not treated as passive activities, which can be relevant for some energy-focused private equity funds.

Partnership Distributions

Distributions from the partnership to its partners can have significant tax implications. The tax treatment depends on whether the distribution is a current (non-liquidating) distribution or a liquidating distribution.

Current Distributions

Current distributions are those made while the partnership continues, and the partner retains an interest in the partnership. The tax treatment of these distributions is as follows:

1. **Cash distributions:**
   a. These are tax-free to the extent of the partner's basis in their partnership interest.
   b. Any excess is generally treated as capital gain.
2. **Property distributions:**
   a. These are generally tax-free.
   b. The partner takes a basis in the distributed property equal to the partnership's basis, but not exceeding the partner's basis in their partnership interest.

Let's look at some examples:

Example 1: Cash distribution. Partner A has a basis of $100,000 in their hedge fund interest. The fund distributes $80,000 to Partner A. Result: The entire $80,000 is tax-free, and Partner A's basis is reduced to $20,000.

Example 2: Cash distribution in excess of basis. Partner B has a basis of $50,000 in their private equity fund interest. The fund distributes $70,000 to Partner B. Result: $50,000 is a tax-free return of basis, and the $20,000 excess is taxable as capital gain. Partner B's basis is reduced to zero.

Example 3: Property distribution. A hedge fund distributes securities with a fair market value of $200,000 and a basis of $150,000 to Partner C, who has a $180,000 basis in their partnership interest. Result: Partner C recognizes no gain on the distribution. Their basis in the securities is $150,000 (the partnership's basis), and their basis in their partnership interest is reduced by $150,000 to $30,000.

Liquidating Distributions

Liquidating distributions occur when a partner's entire interest in the partnership is terminated. This might happen when a partner fully redeems their interest in a hedge fund, or when a private equity fund completes its final distributions and winds up. The tax treatment is as follows:

1. The partner recognizes gain only to the extent that money distributed exceeds the adjusted basis of the partnership interest.
2. Loss can be recognized in certain circumstances (e.g., only cash, unrealized receivables, and inventory are distributed).
3. If property is distributed, the partner's entire remaining basis is allocated to the distributed property.

Example: Liquidating distribution. Partner D has a basis of $500,000 in their private equity fund interest. Upon liquidation of the fund, Partner D receives $450,000 in cash and property with a fair market value of $200,000 and a basis of $100,000. Result:

- Partner D recognizes no gain because the cash received ($450,000) is less than their basis ($500,000).
- Partner D takes a basis of $50,000 in the distributed property (their remaining basis after the cash distribution).
- If Partner D immediately sold the property for its $200,000 fair market value, they would recognize a $150,000 gain.

Sales and Exchanges of Partnership Interests

The sale or exchange of partnership interests is a complex area of tax law that requires careful consideration.

Theoretical Framework

The taxation of partnership interest sales is rooted in the concept of partnership as an aggregate of its partners rather than a distinct entity. This "aggregate theory" influences how the Code treats these transactions, balancing between recognizing the partnership as a separate entity and treating it as a collection of individuals.

General Rule: Capital Gain or Loss

Under section 741 of the Code, the sale or exchange of a partnership interest generally results in capital gain or loss for the selling partner. This treatment aligns with the view that a partnership interest represents an investment in the entity, similar to corporate stock. However, this general rule is subject to several important exceptions and nuances that can significantly impact the tax consequences.

Impact of Liabilities

The treatment of partnership liabilities can significantly impact the tax consequences:

1. **Assumption of liabilities**. When a buyer assumes the selling partner's share of partnership liabilities, it is treated as part of the amount realized.

2. **Relief from liabilities**. The selling partner's relief from their share of partnership liabilities is also considered part of the amount realized.

These rules can sometimes result in taxable gain even when no cash is received, particularly in highly leveraged partnerships.

Calculation of Gain or Loss upon Sale of a Partnership Interest

The basic formula for calculating gain or loss is Amount Realized - Adjusted Basis = Capital Gain or Loss.

1. **Amount realized**. This includes cash, fair market value of property received, and any liabilities assumed by the buyer.
2. **Adjusted basis**. Thid is the partner's basis in their partnership interest, which includes:
   a. Initial capital contributions
   b. Increases for additional contributions and allocated income
   c. Decreases for distributions and allocated losses

Let's look at an example calculation: Consider a scenario where Partner A sells their 25% interest in ABC Partnership to Partner B, who already owns a 25% interest. The partnership has three other partners, each owning 25%.

Partnership details:

- Total partnership assets fair market value: $1,000,000
- Total partnership liabilities: $200,000

Partner A details (seller):

- Adjusted basis in partnership interest: $150,000
- Share of partnership liabilities: $50,000 (25% of $200,000)
- Selling price of interest: $250,000

Tax effects for Partner A (seller):

1. Amount realized:
   a. Cash received: $250,000
   b. Relief from liabilities: $50,000
   c. Total amount realized: $300,000
2. Gain calculation:
   a. Amount realized: $300,000
   b. Adjusted basis: ($150,000)
   c. Total gain: $150,000

Partner A will report $150,000 as capital gain and would get the benefit of long-term capital gain treatment if the investment in the partnership was held for more than one year.

Tax effects for Partner B (buyer):

1. Basis in partnership interest:
   a. Purchase price: $250,000
   b. Assumed share of liabilities: $50,000
   c. Total basis: $300,000

Hot Assets and Ordinary Income

While as a general rule, sales are treated as a capital transaction, section 751 of the Code introduces the concept of "hot assets." These are:

- Unrealized receivables (including recapture items)
- Inventory items

Gain attributable to hot assets is treated as ordinary income, not capital gain. This provision prevents partners from converting ordinary income into capital gain through the sale of their interest.[5]

Section 754 Election and Inside Basis Adjustments

A partnership may make a section 754 election, allowing an adjustment to the inside basis of partnership assets. This election can benefit the purchasing partner by aligning the partnership's internal basis with the price paid for the interest, potentially reducing future taxable gain on asset sales.[6]

The taxation of partnership interest sales and exchanges involves a complex interplay of various Code provisions. While the general rule treats these transactions as capital in nature, numerous exceptions and special rules can result in ordinary income treatment, gain recognition without cash proceeds, or limitations on loss recognition.

Partners and their advisers must carefully analyze these transactions, considering not only the direct tax implications but also the broader impact on the partnership and remaining partners. As with many areas of tax law, the specific facts and circumstances of each case are crucial in determining the ultimate tax treatment.

5. IRC section 751 "hot assets" are beyond the scope of this chapter.
6. IRC section 754 elections are beyond the scope of this chapter.

Tax Reporting to the Investor: Schedule K-1

The Schedule K-1 is a crucial document for investors in partnerships, including those invested in hedge funds and private equity firms. Let's break down what typically appears on a Schedule K-1 and why it is important, and then discuss the significance of the footnotes.

Typical Contents of Schedule K-1

1. Basic information:
    a. Partnership's name, address, and employer identification number
    b. Partner's name, address, and taxpayer identification number
    c. Partner's share of profit, loss, and capital (beginning and end of year percentages)
2. Income items:
    a. Ordinary business income (or loss)
    b. Rental real estate income (or loss)
    c. Other rental income (or loss)
    d. Guaranteed payments
    e. Interest income
    f. Ordinary and qualified dividends
    g. Royalties
    h. Short-term and long-term capital gains (or losses)
    i. Other income (or loss)
3. Deduction items:
    a. Section 179 deduction
    b. Other deductions
4. Tax credits:
    a. Various credits the partnership may have earned
5. Alternative minimum tax (AMT) items:
    a. AMT adjustments and income items
6. Tax-exempt income and nondeductible expenses
7. Distributions:
    a. Cash and property distributions made to the partner
8. Other information:
    a. Partner's share of liabilities
    b. Partner's capital account analysis
    c. Partner's share of partnership's net unrecognized section 704(c) gain or loss

Importance of Schedule K-1

1. **Tax reporting**. The K-1 provides the information needed for the investor to accurately report their share of the partnership's income, deductions, and credits on their personal tax return.
2. **Basis tracking**. It helps investors track their basis in the partnership, which is crucial for determining the tax treatment of distributions and the ability to deduct losses.
3. **Character of income**. It specifies the character of income (e.g., ordinary income, capital gains), which affects the tax rate applied.
4. **AMT calculations**. It provides information necessary for AMT calculations.
5. **Foreign reporting**. For partnerships with foreign investments, it may include information needed for foreign tax credit calculations or other international tax reporting requirements.

Importance of Schedule K-1 Footnotes

1. **Additional context**. Footnotes provide additional context and explanations for the numbers reported on the K-1. They can clarify how certain amounts were calculated or allocated.
2. **Special allocations**. If the partnership uses special allocation methods, the footnotes may explain these, which is crucial for understanding why your share of certain items might differ from your overall ownership percentage.
3. **Tax elections**. The footnotes may disclose certain tax elections made by the partnership that affect how you report your share of partnership items.
4. **Section 704(c) information**. Details about how the partnership handles section 704(c) allocations (related to contributed property with built-in gain or loss) are often found in the footnotes.
5. **Debt information**. Additional details about your share of partnership liabilities, including whether they are recourse or nonrecourse, may be provided in the footnotes.
6. **Foreign reporting requirements**. The footnotes may alert you to potential foreign reporting requirements, such as the need to file Form 8865 (Return of U.S. Persons with Respect to Certain Foreign Partnerships).
7. **State tax information**. Information about state-specific tax treatments or filing requirements is often included in the footnotes.

8. **Carried interest**. For private equity investments, the footnotes may provide information about carried interest allocations and the holding periods of underlying investments, which is crucial given the recent changes to carried interest taxation.
9. **UBTI information**. For tax-exempt investors, the footnotes may provide information about unrelated business taxable income (UBTI), which could trigger tax liabilities.
10. **QBI information**. With the introduction of the qualified business income (QBI) deduction, footnotes may provide information necessary for calculating this deduction.

In essence, while the main body of the K-1 provides the numbers you need, the footnotes often provide the context and additional information you need to understand those numbers and ensure you are using them correctly in a valuation. They can alert you to complex tax situations that might require additional analysis or professional advice.

Given the complexity of partnership taxation, especially for hedge funds and private equity investments, the footnotes should be reviewed for important information.

Difference Between Financial and Tax Reporting

There are significant differences between tax reporting (Schedule K-1) and book capital accounting statements, as follows:

- The K-1 form reports the recipient's share of the partnership's income, deductions, and credits for tax purposes.
- The book capital statement reflects the partnership's financial position based on accounting principles.

This means a partner's taxable income from the partnership may not match the income shown in financial statements. These two reports often show different figures due to varying accounting methods and tax rules.

With respect to financial reporting and book capital, and how this information contrasts with tax reporting and Schedule K-1, differences may arise related to:

- Nontaxable income and nondeductible expenses
- Fair value accounting for transactions
- Tax distributions made by the partnership
- Partnership-level taxes

Let's explore these common book/tax differences further.

Nontaxable Income and Nondeductible Expenses

Gains and losses on investments held by investment partnerships can be divided into "realized" and "unrealized" gains and losses. Investment funds *realize* a gain or a loss when they sell an investment. *Unrealized* gains and losses, often referred to as "paper" gains and losses, represent changes in the value of an investment before it is sold or otherwise exited.

Unrealized gains and losses will generally be the most significant element of nontaxable income for an investment partnership, which is to say that unrealized gains and losses will generally represent one of the most material differences between "tax" and "book" profits and losses. Unrealized gains do not generally give rise to tax liabilities for the partnership or individual partners.

The calculation of unrealized gains and losses for financial reporting will follow applicable accounting principles. For purposes of this discussion of unrealized gains and losses, we will refer to generally accepted accounting principles in the United States (US GAAP). Under US GAAP, investment companies have special accounting rules that require them to account for most investments they hold at fair value, with changes in fair value recorded in profit or loss. US GAAP requires that investment companies initially measure assets and liabilities at fair value, with any difference between the transaction price and fair value recognized immediately as a gain or loss in earnings.

Under US GAAP, fair value is based on a concept of "exit price" (the price that would be received to sell an asset or paid to transfer a liability). The exit price is based on expectations about the exit price from the perspective of market participants. US GAAP requires that a fair value measurement should reflect all of the assumptions that market participants would use in pricing an asset or liability.

Estimation of the fair value of investments, especially illiquid or thinly traded investments, is an inherently subjective exercise. Estimated fair values do not necessarily represent the amounts that may be ultimately realized upon the exit of the investment. Because of the inherent uncertainty of valuation, estimated fair values may be materially higher or lower than the values that may ultimately be realized upon exit of the investment, and the differences could be material. See Figure 13.1 and the chart at the end of the chapter for tables comparing realized and unrealized gains within the tax recognition framework.

Figure 13.1

Hypothetical Example of Unrealized and Realized Gains

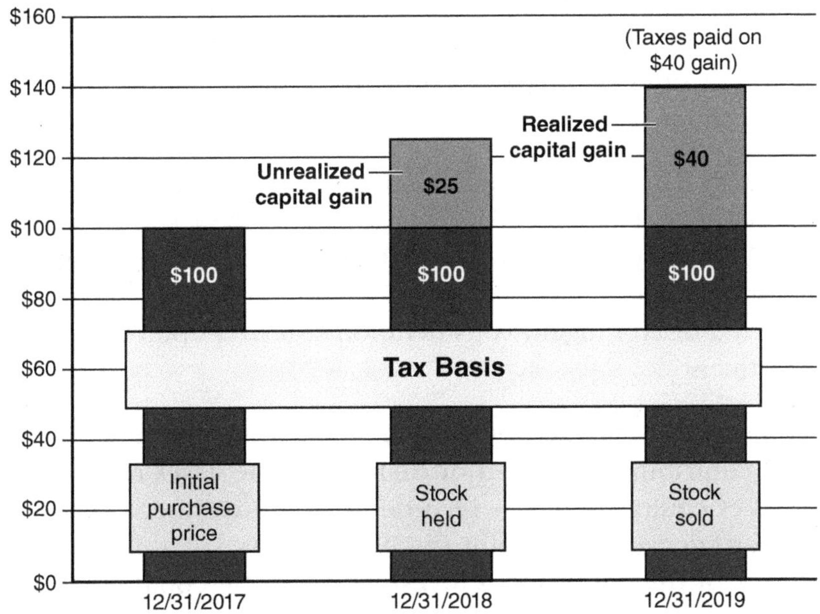

US GAAP recognizes a fair value hierarchy that distinguishes between market data obtained from independent sources (observable inputs) and the investment fund's own market assumptions (unobservable inputs). Investment valuations are classified as Level 1, Level 2, or Level 3, depending on the degree to which unobservable inputs are utilized in the valuation. The reliance on unobservable inputs, and thus the degree of judgment exercised by the investment fund in determining fair value, is greatest for investments categorized in Level 3.

While unrealized gains do not generally give rise to tax liabilities for the partnership or individual partners, fund managers may consider current unrealized gains (or losses) *when calculating the tax consequences of a sale or weighing pros and cons of different investment exit scenarios.*

Expenses like entertainment and life insurance premiums will generally be the most significant element of nondeductible expenses for an investment partnership, which is to say that these expense types will generally represent another difference between "tax" and "book" profits and losses. Nondeductible expenses do not generally give rise to any reduction in the tax liabilities for the partnership or individual partners.

Fair Value Accounting for Transactions

In addition to requiring fair value accounting for open positions (assets and liabilities held on the last day of the accounting period), US GAAP requires that investment funds utilize fair value accounting for other investment-related transactions, such as:

- Non-cash ("in kind") capital contributions and distributions to/from the investment fund
- Certain types of mergers and acquisition activity involving portfolio investments
- Deferred or contingent consideration received upon the sale of an investment

An investment fund may accept securities or other nonmonetary assets as an "in-kind contribution" in lieu of cash. Both the asset received and the contribution of equity should be recorded in the investment fund's financial statements at fair value pursuant to US GAAP. As such, for book reporting, the basis of the contributed investment will be equal to its fair value as determined on the date of the contribution. This is in contrast to tax reporting, which requires that the investment partnership's basis in the contributed asset (known as "inside basis") is the same as the contributing partner's basis.

An investment fund may distribute securities or other nonmonetary assets as an "in-kind distribution" in lieu of cash. Both the asset distributed and the distribution of equity should be recorded in the investment fund's financial statements at fair value pursuant to US GAAP. As such, for book reporting, the investment fund should calculate and record a realized gain or loss equal to the difference between the fair value of the distributed investment as determined on the date of the distribution and the investment fund's basis in the distributed investment (basis as determined in accordance with US GAAP).

Corporate reorganizations (mergers and acquisitions or divisions) involving portfolio investments held by an investment fund may be taxable or nontaxable to shareholders. Corporate reorganizations may be eligible for nonrecognition of gains for tax purposes at the shareholder level. Mergers can be nontaxable if a significant portion of the payment to the target corporation is in stock rather than cash and if substantially all of the assets of the target corporation are acquired. Divisions may be nontaxable if they meet certain conditions designed to ensure that firms are continuing the same business with the same historical shareholders. Even in a generally tax-free reorganization, compensation in cash (called "boot") is taxable.

The US GAAP treatment of a merger or division often follows the same or similar criteria utilized for tax reporting (recognition of realized versus unrealized gains) in order to achieve a result for financial reporting that is consistent with the economic substance of the reorganization transaction.

An investment fund may sell its portfolio investments and receive the proceeds from such disposition in installments ("escrow receivables"). Escrow receivables are generally expected to be funded and available for release to the investment fund based on the requirements in the purchase and sales agreements between the investment fund and the purchasing entities. Upon sale of an investment, an investment fund may receive "contingent consideration." Contingent consideration refers to additional amounts from liquidated investments that management believes may be realized at future dates and/or as future events occur. The terms of these milestones are generally defined in the sales agreements of the liquidated investment. The amount of the actual milestone payments ultimately received by the investment fund may vary depending on whether the future milestone events occur. For financial reporting, pursuant to US GAAP, proceeds anticipated, but not yet received, including escrow receivables and contingent consideration, should be reported at fair value. For financial reporting, fair value of the consideration received upon the sale of the investment, including the fair value of any escrow receivables or contingent consideration, is the relevant input in the calculation of the realized gain or loss on the sale of the portfolio investment.

Tax Distributions

As discussed earlier in this chapter, many investment partnerships have governing documents that contain "carried interest" provisions as a component of the distribution waterfall scheme. These carried interest provisions typically provide that the general partner of the investment partnership will receive a special allocation of fund profits if certain stipulated fund returns are achieved.

Furthermore, many investment funds contain a provision requiring that if, after the fund has made its final liquidating distribution, the general partner has received distributions of carried interest in excess of the amounts that should have been distributed to the general partner as carried interest, the general partner will be obligated to return to the investment fund such excess distributions (a clawback provision).

If permitted by an investment fund's governing documents, an investment fund may make an advance payment to the general partner or its affiliates to discharge a tax liability arising from the general partner's entitlement to carried interest. Such a payment may be called a "tax distribution" and may arise where the general partner is subject to tax in jurisdictions where carried interest is taxed on an accrual basis, which may mean that the tax charge will arise prior to carried interest being paid out. In general, any tax distributions will be deducted from the carried interest to which the general partner is ultimately entitled.

Some investment partnerships include a provision in their governing documents reducing the amount of any clawback by actual, potential, or hypothetical taxes applicable to the general partner or its affiliates. That is to say, these provisions require that any clawback by the investment partnership (and ultimately by the limited partners of the investment partnership) will be net of taxes incurred by the general partner or its affiliates. Said another way, tax distributions may not be subject to clawback if this is specifically stated in the governing documents of the investment partnership.

Managers of investment partnerships should be mindful of these tax scenarios when drafting governing documents of investment partnerships and all partners should understand if any clawbacks reported in the US GAAP financial statements of the investment partnership are net of tax distributions.

Partnership-Level Taxes

As discussed earlier in this chapter, an investment partnership is generally not subject to income taxes and each partner is responsible for the tax liability, if any, related to its proportionate share of the partnership's taxable income. As such, for many investment partnerships, no provision for income taxes is reflected in the US GAAP financial statements.

For financial reporting, pursuant to US GAAP, an investment fund must evaluate its tax positions in accordance with Accounting Standards Codification (ASC) 740, Income Taxes. Specifically, an investment fund must determine whether its tax positions would be sustained upon examination, based on the technical merits of the positions (assuming the taxing authority has full knowledge of all information) based upon a "more-likely-than-not" (MLTN) threshold. If this threshold is not met, none of the tax benefit provided by the position is reflected in the financial statements. For a tax position that meets the MLTN recognition threshold, the benefit is measured at the largest amount of benefit that is greater than 50% likely of being realized upon ultimate settlement. Additionally, related interest and penalties, if any, should be recorded in accordance with ASC 740, for financial reporting.

Certain scenarios that may give rise to a tax liability (or tax asset) at the investment partnership level are as follows:

- Trade or business or effectively connected income
- Use of taxable blockers or special purpose vehicles within the fund structure
- State-level taxes, pass-through entity taxes
- Foreign taxes on dividends or capital gains on portfolio investments
- IRS recourse to partnerships resulting from Bipartisan Budget Act (and availability of pushout election, etc.)
- Investor withholding tax considerations

Summary

This chapter followed an AAM's tax and accounting life cycle from formation to exit. It opened with the pass-through framework that governs hedge fund and private equity partnerships, showing how income keeps its character as it flows to partners and why "phantom income" and careful basis tracking are unavoidable. After contrasting this single-layer regime with the double taxation of C corporations, the discussion turned to the partnership agreement's economic engine: capital accounts, distribution waterfalls, special allocations, and the carried interest rules that now demand a three-year holding period under section 1061.

We then examined cash, property, and service contributions under section 721, the ongoing basis adjustments created by income, losses, liabilities, and distributions, and the additional limits imposed by basis, at-risk, and passive activity rules. Current and liquidating distributions received a close look, as did sales of partnership interests, the ordinary-income sting of hot assets, and the optional section 754 step-up that can realign inside and outside basis. A detailed review of Schedule K-1 explained what investors actually report, followed by an exploration of the book/tax divide that arises from fair value accounting, unrealized gains, nondeductible expenses, tax distributions, and partnership-level exposures under ASC 740.

Realized vs. Unrealized Gains

Conceptual Framework for Tax Recognition

Unrealized Gain	Realized Gain
Economic appreciation in asset value	Gain fixed through taxable transaction
No recognition event has occurred	Recognition event has occurred
No current tax liability	**Tax liability triggered (subject to applicable rules)**
Paper gain only	Actual disposition of property

Illustrative Example: Stock Appreciation and Sale

Event	Asset Value	Gain Status	Tax Consequence
Year 1: Purchase stock	$10,000	None (basis)	No tax event
Year 3: Stock appreciates	$25,000	$15,000 unrealized	No recognition; no tax
Year 5: Stock continues to appreciate	$32,000	$22,000 unrealized	No recognition; no tax
Year 6: Sale of stock	$32,000	**$22,000 realized**	**Recognition event; tax due***

*Subject to applicable tax rates, holding period rules, and available deductions or exclusions.

Key Tax Principles

Principle	Explanation
Realization Requirement	Under IRC § 1001, gain or loss is recognized upon a sale or exchange of property. Mere appreciation does not trigger tax liability.
Amount Realized	The sum of money received plus the fair market value of property received in the transaction (IRC § 1001(b)).
Adjusted Basis	Generally, the cost of the property, adjusted for depreciation, improvements, or other modifications (IRC § 1012, § 1016).
Gain Recognition	Gain = Amount Realized minus Adjusted Basis. Recognition typically follows realization unless a nonrecognition provision applies.
Timing	Tax is imposed in the year of the realization event, not during the period of appreciation.

Common Realization Events

Transaction Type	Recognition Status
Sale to third party	Realized gain; generally recognized immediately unless exception applies
Exchange of property	Realized gain; may be deferred under IRC § 1031 (like-kind exchange) on real property held for investment or other nonrecognition provisions
Distribution to shareholder	Realized gain at corporate level (generally); taxable to extent of fair market value
Gift or inheritance	No realization to donor; recipient takes carryover or stepped-up basis under IRC § 1015 or § 1014
Mere holding of property	No realization; appreciation remains unrealized regardless of duration or magnitude

Note: This chart provides a general framework. Specific tax treatment depends on applicable statutory provisions, regulations, and the particular facts of each transaction. Special rules may apply for certain asset types, transactions, and taxpayer classifications.

Appendix A

Common Terms Used in Hedge Funds and Private Equity Firms

In this appendix the readers will become familiar with many terms commonly referred to in the analysis and valuation of alternative asset management firms. If one is to understand a valuation report on the various interests that comprise an alternative asset management firm, they must be familiar with these terms.

Private equity (PE) firms use a variety of terms and jargon specific to the industry. Here are some commonly used terms:

1. **Activist Fund: See the description and key points at the end of the appendix.**
2. **Add-On Acquisition**: The acquisition of additional companies or assets by a portfolio company that are integrated into the portfolio company to grow its business. An add-on acquisition is also referred to as a bolt-on acquisition.
3. **Bridge Financing**: Short-term financing used to meet immediate funding needs until more permanent (long-term) financing can be secured
4. **Buyout**: The acquisition of a company, often using a combination of equity and significant amounts of borrowed money (leverage)
5. **Capital Call**: A request by the general partner (GP) for a portion of the committed capital from the limited partners (LPs) for fund investments and/or expenses
6. **Carried Interest (Carry)**: The share of the profits that the GP receives from the fund's investment returns, typically around 20%
7. **Committed Capital**: The total amount of capital that LPs agree to contribute to a PE fund
8. **Deal Flow**: The rate at which investment opportunities are presented to a firm
9. **Distressed Investing**: Investing in companies or assets that are in financial difficulty, typically at a significant discount

10. **Distribution Waterfall**: A mechanism, generally found in a PE fund's limited partnership agreement, through which investment returns are allocated between LPs and the GP
11. **Distribution Waterfall (American Style)**: A distribution waterfall that distributes investment proceeds on a deal-by-deal basis
12. **Distribution Waterfall (European Style)**: A distribution waterfall that distributes investment proceeds after the entire fund meets its preferred return threshold
13. **Dry Powder**: Capital that has been committed by LPs but has not yet been invested by the GP
14. **Due Diligence**: The comprehensive appraisal of a business by a prospective buyer, particularly in terms of its assets, liabilities, and commercial potential
15. **European Waterfall**: A distribution structure where the GP receives carried interest only after all contributed capital and a preferred return have been fully returned to LPs
16. **Exit Strategy**: The method by which a PE firm intends to sell its investment in a company, such as through an initial public offering (IPO), sale to another company (trade sale), or sale to another PE firm (secondary buyout)
17. **Fund of Funds**: A fund that invests in other PE funds rather than directly in companies
18. **Fund Term or Life**: Duration of a fund's term specified in the fund's partnership agreement; contractually limited, usually to ten years with one or two one-year extensions
19. **General Partner (GP)**: The entity responsible for making day-to-day decisions on behalf of the PE fund, and raising capital/making capital calls. The GP assumes all legal liability. The GP can also be referred to as the fund manager. The GP is typically compensated if certain performance benchmarks are achieved in the form of carried interest. Note, in the absence of a standalone management company, the GP may take on all of the management company's responsibilities (see below) and receive a management fee from the funds.
20. **Harvesting Period**: The period of a PE fund's life cycle where the GP will focus on growing the portfolio companies, including making add-on acquisitions, and then realizing/exiting the investments. Investment proceeds are allocated between the GP and LPs based upon the fund's distribution waterfall.
21. **Internal Rate of Return (IRR)**: A metric used to evaluate the profitability of an investment, representing the annualized rate of return

22. **Invested Capital**: The total amount of capital that has been invested in portfolio companies and to cover fund expenses
23. **Investment Period**: The period of a PE fund's life cycle where investments are made using capital called by the GP in accordance with the fund's investment strategy
24. **Leveraged Buyout (LBO)**: A buyout in which a significant portion of the purchase price is financed through debt
25. **Limited Partner (LP)**: Investors in the fund. They provide capital but do not have a role in managing the investments.
26. **Management Company**: An operating entity responsible for employing investment professionals and other employees, making investment decisions, overseeing/maintaining fund investments, and paying the expenses in connection with managing the funds. The management company is typically compensated for its services through management fees.
27. **Management Fee**: The annual fee, usually expressed as a percentage of assets under management, paid by the fund to the management company for managing the fund. In private equity, management fee is typically calculated as a percentage of the committed capital during the investment period and as a percentage of invested capital during the harvesting period.
28. **Management Fee Offset**: A reduction to a contractual management fee equal to all or a portion of ancillary fees, such as investment banking fees, monitoring fees, and so on, that a management entity may earn directly from the fund's portfolio companies.
29. **Management Fee Waivers**: Fund agreements typically allow PE/venture capital (VC) firms to waive a portion of management fees in exchange for LPs funding a portion of the fund GP's capital commitment. LPs still make capital contributions for the amount of waived fees, but the contributed capital is invested in the fund on behalf of the PE/VC firm's principals.
30. **Multiple of Invested Capital (MOIC)**: A measure of the total value, both realized and unrealized, of an investment compared to the amount of capital invested
31. **Portfolio Company**: A company in which a fund has invested
32. **Preferred Return/Hurdle Rate**: The minimum required rate of return that a fund must achieve before the GP can share in the investment proceeds/profits
33. **Private Placement Memorandum (PPM)**: A fund's marketing document that provides an overview of the fund and discloses the investment terms (including fees), investment strategy and

methodologies, target market, background of the principals and investment team, investment track record, potential risks, tax and regulatory disclosures, and subscription procedures. This document is also called a confidential offering memorandum (COM).

34. **Residual Value to Paid-In Capital (RVPI)**: A metric used in PE and VC to measure the unrealized value of a fund's holdings relative to the total amount of capital invested (paid-in capital) by the investors. Essentially, RVPI indicates the value of a fund's remaining assets that have not yet been realized or distributed to investors.
35. **Return on Invested Capital**: A way to assess a company's efficiency at allocating the capital under its control to profitable investments
36. **Secondaries**: The buying and selling of preexisting investor commitments to PE funds
37. **Total Value to Paid-In Capital (TVPI)**: A key performance metric used in PE and VC investing. It measures the ratio of the current value of a fund's holdings plus distributions to the total amount of capital invested (paid-in capital) by the investors. In simpler terms, TVPI indicates the overall value generated by the investment relative to the amount of capital invested in it.
38. **Uncalled Capital**: The amount of committed capital that has not been called by the fund's GP

Hedge funds, like PE firms, have a unique set of terminology that is frequently used within the industry. Here are some commonly used terms associated with hedge funds:

1. **Absolute Return**: The return that a hedge fund achieves without comparison to any benchmark index
2. **Accredited Investor**: An individual or entity that meets specific financial criteria, allowing them to invest in hedge funds and other private investment vehicles
3. **Activist Fund: See the description and key points at the end of the appendix.**
4. **Alpha**: A measure of the performance of a hedge fund relative to a benchmark index, representing the value that a fund manager adds to or subtracts from the investment
5. **Arbitrage Strategy**: An investment strategy that pursues pricing inefficiencies and market mispricing to seek a profit
6. **Assets Under Management (AUM)**: The total market value of the capital managed by an investment firm
7. **Beta**: A measure of the volatility or systematic risk of a hedge fund relative to the market or a benchmark index

8. **Distressed Securities**: Financial instruments issued by companies in financial distress, which hedge funds may invest in as part of a distressed investing strategy
9. **Drawdown**: The decline in value from a hedge fund's peak to its lowest point during a specific period
10. **Event-Driven Strategy**: An investment strategy that seeks to profit from corporate events such as mergers, acquisitions, bankruptcies, and restructurings
11. **Fee-Paying AUM**: The portion of AUM subject to management and performance fees
12. **Fund of Funds**: An investment fund that invests in other hedge funds
13. **Gate**: A prohibition on the maximum amount of AUM or investor's capital that can be redeemed at one time. It is used to prevent a "run on the bank."
14. **Hedge**: A strategy used to offset or mitigate risk in an investment portfolio
15. **High-Water Mark**: A threshold above which a hedge fund manager earns performance fees. It ensures that investors do not pay performance fees on gains that merely offset prior losses.
16. **High-Water Mark (Modified)**: A modification to the standard high-water mark provision, which allows a manager to receive lower amounts of incentive compensation while the fund is below its high-water mark
17. **Hurdle Rate**: A minimum rate of return that a hedge fund must achieve before the manager can earn performance fees
18. **Leverage**: The use of borrowed capital to increase the potential return of an investment. Hedge funds often use leverage to amplify returns.
19. **Lock-Up Period**: The initial period during which investors cannot redeem or withdraw their investments from the hedge fund
20. **Long-Only Strategy**: An investment strategy where a hedge fund only takes long positions in securities it deems to be undervalued
21. **Long-Short Equity Strategy**: An investment strategy where a hedge fund takes both long positions in securities it deems to be undervalued and short positions in securities it deems to be overvalued
22. **Management Fee**: An asset-based fee charged by the hedge fund manager for managing the fund, usually expressed as a percentage of AUM
23. **Market Neutral**: An investment strategy that seeks to minimize market risk by taking offsetting long and short positions

24. **Net Asset Value (NAV)**: The value of a hedge fund's assets minus its liabilities, often used to measure the per-share value of the fund
25. **Non-Fee-Paying AUM**: The portion of AUM not subject to management and performance fees
26. **Performance Fee**: A fee charged by the hedge fund manager based on the fund's performance, typically a percentage of the profits. A performance fee is also referred to as an incentive fee.
27. **Prime Broker**: A specialized financial intermediary, such as a brokerage firm, that provides various services to hedge funds, such as trade execution, asset custody, financing, and securities lending
28. **Private Placement Memorandum (PPM)**: A document that provides an overview of the hedge fund and discloses the investment terms (including fees), investment strategy and methodologies, target market, background of the principals and investment team, investment track record, potential risks, tax and regulatory disclosures, and subscription procedures. This document is also called a confidential offering memorandum (COM).
29. **Quantitative Strategy (Quant)**: An investment strategy that relies on mathematical models and algorithms to make trading decisions
30. **Redemption**: The process by which an investor withdraws their capital from a hedge fund
31. **Relative Value**: An investment strategy that seeks to exploit price differences between related financial instruments
32. **Residual Value to Paid-In Capital (RVPI)**: A metric used in PE and VC to measure the unrealized value of a fund's holdings relative to the total amount of capital invested (paid-in capital) by the investors. Essentially, RVPI indicates the value of a fund's remaining assets that have not yet been realized or distributed to investors.
33. **Short-Only Strategy**: An investment strategy where a hedge fund only takes short positions in securities it deems to be undervalued
34. **Short Selling**: The practice of selling borrowed securities with the intention of buying them back at a lower price
35. **Side Letter**: An agreement executed by both the hedge fund and an investor that modifies the rights of that investor. Examples of modifications include, but are not limited to, a lower management fee charged to the investor, changing the lock-up period, and lowering the performance fee.
36. **Side Pocket**: A mechanism used to segregate illiquid or hard-to-value assets within a hedge fund
37. **Soft Close/Hard Close**: The temporary (soft close) or permanent (hard close) closure of a hedge fund to new investors

38. **Total Value to Paid-In Capital (TVPI)**: A key performance metric used in PE and VC investing. It measures the ratio of the current value of a fund's holdings plus distributions to the total amount of capital invested (paid-in capital) by the investors. In simpler terms, TVPI indicates the overall value generated by the investment relative to the amount of capital that has been put into the fund.
39. **Withdrawal/Redemption**: A withdrawal from a hedge fund typically requires notice (i.e., 30–90 days) and may be subject to restrictions on the frequency (i.e., monthly, quarterly, etc.) that a withdrawal may be made. Gate and lock-up provisions are common.

VC has its own set of specialized terminology that is frequently used within the industry. Here are some commonly used terms associated with VC:

1. **Activist Fund: See the description and key points at the end of the appendix.**
2. **Angel Investor**: An individual who provides capital for a startup, often in exchange for convertible debt or ownership equity
3. **Bridge Financing**: Short-term financing used to meet immediate funding needs until more permanent (long-term) financing can be secured
4. **Burn Rate**: The rate at which a startup spends its cash reserves to cover overhead before generating positive cash flow
5. **Cap Table (Capitalization Table)**: A spreadsheet or table that shows the ownership stakes, equity dilution, and value of equity in each round of investment for a company
6. **Capital Call**: A request by the GP for a portion of the committed capital from the LPs for fund investments and/or expenses
7. **Carried Interest (Carry)**: The share of the profits that the GP receives from the fund's investment returns, typically around 20%
8. **Convertible Note**: A type of short-term debt that converts into equity, typically during a future financing round
9. **Cumulative Distributions**: The total amount of cash or stock that has been returned to the investors
10. **Dilution**: The reduction in ownership percentage of existing shareholders when new shares are issued
11. **Distributions to Paid-In Capital (DPI)**: A ratio that measures the amount of distributions (cash or stock) a fund has returned to its investors (LPs) relative to the amount of capital they have invested (paid-in capital). It is a measure of realized returns, providing insight into how much cash (or stock) has been returned to investors compared to their original investment.

12. **Down Round**: A funding round in which a company raises capital at a lower valuation than in previous rounds
13. **Drag-Along Rights**: A provision that allows majority shareholders to force minority shareholders to join in the sale of a company
14. **Due Diligence**: The comprehensive appraisal of a business by a prospective investor, especially in terms of its assets, liabilities, and commercial potential
15. **Exit Strategy**: The method by which a VC firm plans to sell its stake in a company, such as through an IPO or acquisition
16. **General Partner (GP)**: The entity or individual responsible for managing the VC fund and making investment decisions
17. **Initial Public Offering (IPO)**: The process of offering shares of a private corporation to the public in a new stock issuance
18. **Limited Partner (LP)**: Investors who provide capital to a VC fund but do not have a role in managing the investments
19. **Paid-In Capital**: The total amount of capital that has been drawn down (called) from the investors by the fund
20. **Pivot**: A significant change in a company's business model or strategy, often based on market feedback or other insights
21. **Post-Money Valuation**: The value of a company after receiving new funding
22. **Pre-Money Valuation**: The value of a company before receiving new funding
23. **Private Placement Memorandum (PPM)**: A document that provides an overview of the VC fund and discloses the investment terms (including fees), investment strategy and methodologies, target market, background of the principals and investment team, investment track record, potential risks, tax and regulatory disclosures, and subscription procedures. This document is also called a confidential offering memorandum (COM).
24. **Pro Rata Rights**: The right of existing investors to maintain their percentage ownership in a company by buying a proportional number of shares in future funding rounds
25. **Residual Value to Paid-In Capital (RVPI)**: Measures the unrealized value of the portfolio relative to the paid-in capital
26. **Runway**: The amount of time a company can operate before it runs out of money, given its current burn rate
27. **Seed Capital**: The initial funding used to start a business, often coming from the founders' personal assets or friends and family
28. **Series A, B, C, etc.**: Different rounds of funding that a startup might go through as it grows. Series A is typically the first round of institutional funding, followed by Series B, C, and so on.

29. **Tag-Along Rights**: A provision that allows minority shareholders to sell their shares on the same terms as the majority shareholders
30. **Term Sheet**: A nonbinding agreement outlining the basic terms and conditions under which an investment will be made
31. **Total Value to Paid-In Capital (TVPI)**: The sum of DPI and RVPI, giving a comprehensive view of the fund's performance by including both realized and unrealized returns
32. **Valuation**: The process of determining the current worth of a company, often based on its potential for future earnings
33. **Vesting**: The process by which an employee earns the right to receive equity over time

Activist Fund: Activist fund investing is a strategy used by individuals or groups (often hedge funds or institutional investors) to buy a significant minority stake in a public company with the goal of influencing its management and operations. Here are some key points about activist investing:

1. **Objectives**: Activist investors aim to bring changes that they believe will increase the company's value. These changes can range from restructuring the company's operations, altering its capital structure, improving corporate governance, influencing management decisions, or even pushing for the sale or merger of the company.
2. **Methods**: Activist investors use various methods to exert their influence, including:
   a. Engaging in private negotiations with the company's management
   b. Proposing changes at shareholder meetings
   c. Launching public campaigns to gain support from other shareholders
   d. Seeking seats on the company's board of directors
3. **Tactics**: Some common tactics used by activist investors include:
   a. Writing open letters to the board of directors or shareholders
   b. Conducting media campaigns to rally public and investor support
   c. Filing shareholder resolutions or proxy fights to gain control over the board
4. **Risks and Rewards**: While activist investing can lead to substantial gains if the proposed changes are successful and increase the company's value, it also carries risks. The targeted company might resist changes, leading to prolonged battles and potential negative impacts on stock prices.
5. **Examples**: Notable activist investors include Carl Icahn, Bill Ackman, and Paul Singer. These investors have a history of taking substantial stakes in companies and pushing for significant changes.

6. **Impact**: Activist investors can have a profound impact on companies. While they often push for changes that might lead to short-term gains, there is debate over whether their actions result in long-term value creation or merely disrupt the company's strategy and operations.
7. **Regulation**: Activist investors must adhere to regulations set by securities authorities, including disclosure requirements when they acquire a significant stake in a company.

In essence, activist investing is about using equity ownership to influence a company's direction and unlock shareholder value, often leading to significant shifts in how the company operates and is managed.

Appendix B

Example of a Document Request List

To value an ownership interest in a private equity or hedge fund, financial and legal information needs to be gathered through a request. The initial document and information request should identify the interests being valued and the date of valuation so that documents can be provided up to that date. A typical document and information request for private equity or hedge funds might include the following:

- Ownership agreements (e.g., partnership/limited liability company (LLC)/limited partnership (LP) agreement) for the LP investment funds, management company, and general partner (GP) entities
- Private placement (or offering) memorandum for investors
- Subscription documents with investors
- Most recent letters, reports, and other financial information sent to investors for investment performance
- Externally prepared financial statements (e.g., audited financial statements) for the investment funds for the previous five years
- Most recent accrual basis balance sheets for the management company and GP entities
- Federal and state income tax returns for the management company for the previous five years
- Management agreements and contracts in effect as of the date of valuation
- Budgets and forecasts prepared in the previous two years
- Calculations of management and incentive fees for the previous five years
- All business valuation reports and calculations for all the companies that have been prepared for any reason in the past five years
- Fee-paying assets under management (AUM) balances and high-water marks by investor class as of the date of valuation
- Schedules showing the waterfall calculations allocating carried interest to the GP; these schedules will likely show the amount of limited partner contributed capital, distributions, preferred return calculation, allocation of expenses, and the hypothetical distribution of the fair value of fund investments as of the date of valuation

- Annual employee base and bonus compensation (Form W-2 wages and allocated incentive fees by employee/owner) for the previous five years
- Gross and net investment returns on a monthly or annual basis from inception through the date of valuation based upon a representative investor class
- Capital account statements as of the date of valuation
- Quantification of subscriptions and redemptions for the previous five years
- Fund structure chart

Index